Diablo –
In the Valley of Tears

Gabi Adam

Diablo –
In the Valley of Tears

Copyright: © Gabi Adam 2009
Original title: Im Tal der Tränen
Cover photo: © Bob Langrish
Cover layout: Stabenfeldt AS

Typeset by Roberta L. Melzl
Editor: Bobbie Chase
Printed in Germany, 2009

ISBN: 978-1-934983-22-5

Stabenfeldt, Inc.
225 Park Avenue South
New York, NY 10003
www.pony4kids.com

Available exclusively through PONY.

Chapter 1

Fifteen-year-old Ricki Sulai sat at the breakfast table, staring straight ahead listlessly and picking at her blueberry muffin.

"What's wrong with you today?" her mother, Brigitte, asked. "It's Saturday. The sun is shining, it looks like it's going to be a beautiful day, and you haven't stepped outside yet but you're already in a bad mood. So what is it?"

"You're not always in a good mood either."

"That's true, but I try not to take it out on others."

Ricki rolled her eyes and groaned.

"I'm trying, but if Harry turned on his radio full blast at 4:30 in the morning and you almost fell out of bed, you'd be mad, too, wouldn't you?"

Brigitte looked over at Ricki's younger brother.

"You did WHAT? At 4:30 in the morning!?"

Harry just shrugged his shoulders as he poured the milk over his corn flakes so quickly that a lot of it spilled onto the table.

"Oops," he said, as Ricki jumped up to get out of the way of the liquid dripping off the table.

"Harry! Watch what you're doing, you idiot!" she yelled at him and received a disapproving look from her mother.

"Ricki! Please don't use that tone! That could happen to anyone," she admonished.

"But it happens to this idiot every morning!"

"That's not true!" Harry tried to sop up the puddle of milk with a paper napkin, which didn't work very well.

"This mess is revolting," complained Ricki. "Can't you get a kitchen sponge?"

"Nope!"

"Harry, get the sponge," his mother ordered him, and the youngster jumped up.

"Okay! I was just going to get it anyway," he remarked with a sweet smile.

Ricki looked at her brother, shook her head contemptuously, and got up.

"This is so annoying, I'm going over to the stable."

"Would you please put your dishes in the sink before you go?" Brigitte pointed at the table. "You often leave everything on the table, and you're old enough now to realize that one should –"

"Yeah, Ricki. Clear your plate!"

"Oh, be quiet, Harry, and mind your own business!" Ricki hastily reached for her plate and cup and put both into the sink, and then she rushed out of the kitchen before her mother could remember that it was her turn to do the breakfast dishes.

On her way out, she stopped at the coat rack in the hallway to grab her jacket, and then slipped into a pair of old sneakers. She took an apple from the large bowl of fruit on the hall bureau and reached for the doorknob.

"Rosie!" called Ricki and whistled softly. "Rosie, come!"

She didn't need to call twice. Ricki's dog came bounding down the stairs and jumped up on the girl happily.

"Hey, don't be so rough. Wait a minute, girl, I have to open the door first!"

Rosie ran outside immediately and then back and forth across the yard, before devoting her attention to the chipmunks in their holes, sniffing and wagging her tail.

Shivering, Ricki zipped up her jacket and squinted her eyes in the rising morning sun, proclaiming it a wonderful day in spite of the chill in the spring air.

Ricki loved these hours in the early morning, although she had to force herself to get out of her warm bed. However, once she stood outside and filled her lungs with fresh air, she always felt terrific. As she let her gaze wander across the beautiful landscape that surrounded her parents' old farmhouse, life seemed wonderful, and her bothersome kid brother was quickly forgotten.

As she did every morning, the teenager ran over to the stable. Just the thought of her Diablo, who would soon greet her with a loud whinny, put her in a great mood. The big, black gelding had fulfilled Ricki's dream of a horse of her own, and she could never imagine life without him.

Carefully she opened the latch of the stable's divided door, and as she folded the door back, the familiar warm scent of horses filled her nostrils. For a moment Ricki shut her eyes to savor this morning ritual before entering the stable, where the snorting, whinnying, and braying horse-and-donkey-version of "good morning" greeted her.

"Hello, my darlings! Everything okay?" She went quickly from one stall to the next and patted each of the animals on the neck, before giving Diablo a kiss on his warm nose and offering him an apple.

"Good morning," she said softly. "Did you sleep well? You're all probably hungry, aren't you? Just wait a bit. I'm going to bring you something in a minute."

With one last glance at her beloved black horse she ran over to the feed storeroom and prepared the portions of oats, mixed with a little vitamin powder and enriched feed, for each animal.

Doc Holliday thundered against the stall wall with his hoof. As usual, her girlfriend Lillian Bates's white horse couldn't wait for his breakfast.

"Holli, be quiet!" shouted Ricki into the corridor, and then hurried back, carrying three buckets at a time to feed all six four-legged friends.

What a wonderful feeling it was to be up and about in the morning in her own stable. She had always wished for this and had been so happy when her dream had finally been realized. It had been quite a while now, but she never took her good fortune for granted.

Once the animals stood in their stalls munching contentedly, Ricki opened a new bale of hay and grabbed a pitchfork, so she could fill the racks, one after the other.

"Sharazan, get your head out of the way! ... Rashid, don't be so greedy! ... Hey, Salina, if you don't move out of the way, I can't get to the rack. Man, you're so stubborn today, worse than a donkey – Oh, Chico, excuse me, I didn't mean anything by that," laughed Ricki, as Lillian's little donkey, who shared a stall with the pony mare Salina, looked at her as though she was offended by her words.

When Ricki finished feeding the animals she decided to start mucking out the stalls. She was sure Jake, the Sulais' elderly stableman, would appear in the next few minutes and wouldn't mind if she did some of his work for him in the meantime. After all, as he kept reminding her and her friends, he wasn't getting any younger.

Once again Ricki regretted that she could only help out in the stable on the weekends. During the week, she had only a few minutes between getting up and breakfast, and all she could do was greet Diablo before she had to leave for school.

While she was cleaning out Sharazan's stall, she thought of her boyfriend, Kevin Thomas, to whom the roan belonged. All of a sudden she remembered the dream she'd had the night before, which had been the real reason for her bad mood at breakfast. Harry's early-morning musical wake-up call had been the last straw, since she'd been trying to get back to sleep after dreaming that Kevin had broken up with her.

Ricki stroked Sharazan affectionately across his mane.

"Let's hope that stupid dream doesn't become reality, or you probably won't be in this stable much longer," she whispered to him.

Pushing the wheelbarrow along toward Rashid's stall next, Ricki soon forgot about the dream.

Rashid and Salina both belonged to the former circus equestrienne Carlotta Mancini, who had established Mercy Ranch for retired, abused, and unwanted horses, and the young friends loved riding over there. Ricki's friend Cathy

Sutherland took care of Rashid. Just like Kevin and Lillian, she came to the stable almost every afternoon. All things considered, Ricki thought it was great that her friends' horses were in her family's stable, and there was hardly a day when the teens didn't go riding, hang out and talk, or do something else together.

"Good morning, Ricki," Jake said, entering the stable and yawning heartily. "Can I go back to sleep now or did you leave some work for me to do?"

"Hi, Jake!" Ricki peered around Rashid. "I just started to cart out the manure. Sharazan's stall is done."

The old man nodded.

"Then if you give me the pitchfork, I'll get started."

"Okay."

"If you want to do something more, you could throw down a couple of bales of straw. You know, I'm starting to have some trouble climbing the ladder up to the hayloft."

"No problem, Jake. I'll be glad to do it. Oh, I want to ask you something. Has Lupo disappeared? I haven't seen him in a long time." Ricki had missed the stable tomcat for several days and was worried about him.

"Oh, him? He's fine! He's just gotten used to spending more time on my bed than outside!" laughed Jake. "When I put him outside, five minutes later he's back, meowing tragically under the window until I let him inside."

Ricki grinned.

"He's discovered that it's easier to wait until you open the refrigerator than it is to chase after the mice in the stable."

"Exactly! Rosie's much better at chasing mice," the old man replied and started working, while Ricki took care of the bales of straw.

It was about one o'clock when Lillian, Kevin, and Cathy arrived at the Sulais' stable to saddle their horses with Ricki and head over to Echo Lake to meet up with some riders from Mercy Ranch.

When the four arrived at the lake, Beth, Logan, Cheryl, and Hal were already there, waving to them from a distance.

"Hey, you guys are right on time!" Beth called out as she shortened her reins on Rondo. When her horse saw the other riders approaching he began to skitter from side to side.

"We try!" Ricki nodded to her and smiled warmly at Logan. Just a short while ago there had been a lot of tension between the two of them, because Ricki didn't trust Beth's boyfriend – in fact she had disliked him a lot. But she had discovered that she misjudged him and that Logan was really a good guy after all, so they were able to patch things up.

Hal rode over beside Cathy right away, and old Jonah, whom he was riding, greeted Rashid enthusiastically by rubbing his head on the other horse's neck.

Hal was always glad to see Cathy, and hoped that in time their relationship would become closer once he regained her trust, and she came to know how important she was to him. He was truly sorry that he had broken up with her in order to go out with an awful girl named Lena.

Cheryl was riding Sheila, a Black Forest Shire mare she had fallen in love with at first sight. Now she took care of Sheila at Mercy Ranch. Just like most of the people who have foster horses, she dreamed that one day Sheila would belong to her.

"Have you been waiting long?" asked Kevin.

"No," answered Logan.

"Yeah!" Hal responded.

"Oh, okay!" Lillian grinned at the two boys.

"Well, five minutes isn't really a long time, but when I'm waiting for Cathy, every second seems like an eternity!" Hal winked at Rashid's rider, obviously smitten.

"Romeo has spoken!" Kevin nodded sympathetically. "I used to feel like that, too."

"Ouch!" Ricki looked at him questioningly. "But not any more?"

"Oh, did I say something wrong?" The boy looked at her innocently.

"Hey, you guys, our stable is almost finished and Star is moving into his stall the beginning of next week." Logan patted his white Arabian on the neck.

"Wow! Next week, already?" Beth looked surprised.

"Don't look so stunned! My offer still stands. You can see the stable for yourself and, if you like it, you can board Rondo there, too. We have four stalls and want to rent three of them anyway, so that Star has company."

"Yeah, I know. I think it's great, and the idea that Rondo would be with Star is fantastic, but I'll miss Carlotta. I've gotten so used to Mercy Ranch," replied Beth, somewhat sadly, but she knew that Rondo and Star were only temporary guests at the ranch. The stalls there were for old or formerly abused and neglected horses. She should be glad that when Rondo left there would be a stall available for some poor animal who could spend the rest of his life in peace on Mercy Ranch.

"I feel the same way," Logan had to admit. "Carlotta is the best! But having your own stable is nice too."

"That's true," Ricki nodded in agreement. "Where is the stable? Is it far from here?"

Logan shook his head. "We live about half an hour away."

"Then there's no problem," Lillian said to Beth. "It's so close you can ride over to the ranch whenever you want to."

"You're right." Beth's face brightened. "Hey, Logan, can we go see your stable right now?"

"Oh, yeah! I'd like to see it, too!" Cathy looked at Logan pleadingly.

"Sure! Why not? Let's all ride over to my house." He laughed. "My mother wants to meet the people I spend so much time with anyway."

"Then what are we waiting for? I can't wait to see it."

***

Carlotta stood in front of one of the broad paddocks on Mercy Ranch and observed her horses grazing contentedly. It was always a wonderful sight for her, no matter how often she went here, and the peacefulness of the idyllic scene swept over her.

Of course, the ranch was a lot of work, and it wasn't exactly cheap to maintain, but even though Carlotta had to cut corners toward the end of each month to keep the ranch out of debt, she knew there would never be anything more important to her than keeping the place going so the horses could enjoy the rest of their lives here in comfort.

At the moment she was thinking about the fact that soon Star and Rondo would no longer be at the ranch, which would mean that the two sources of income from their stall rents would be gone. This wouldn't make the financial situation any easier.

Once again she reminded herself that, for a long time now, she had thought about finding a good home for Sheila. After all, under Carlotta and Cheryl's care Sheila had rid herself of her mistrust for people and now she was a very reliable horse. She was completely healthy, not yet old, and a wonderful horse to ride. It wouldn't be difficult to find a buyer for her, but nevertheless, Carlotta would examine prospective buyers closely to make sure the horse ended up in good hands.

She sighed.

It will break Cheryl's heart, she thought despondently, and she had to admit to herself that she, too, had become so fond of Sheila that it would be hard for her to let the horse go. She would have liked to keep all the horses at the ranch forever but, unfortunately, that wasn't possible. And with the extremely tight financial situation right now, she had no other choice but to part with Sheila.

With a heavy heart, the ranch owner turned away from the paddock and went back to her house, where she sat down at her desk in the office.

She opened a drawer and took out a piece of paper on which she had written out an advertisement for Sheila just a few days ago, and which she had already called in to the newspaper.

Wearily she leaned her elbows on her desk and covered her face with her hands. She felt as if she had betrayed a friend.

***

"Happy birthday to you, happy birthday to you! Happy birthday, dear Marisa, happy birthday to youuuuu!"
Patrick and Mona Swinton sang the birthday song for their

daughter pretty badly, but with all their hearts. Marisa was fifteen years old today, and she could hardly keep herself from laughing.

"You didn't practice that much, did you?" she grinned, and responded to the warm hug her father gave her, which almost cut off her air supply.

"Happy birthday, my darling Marisa. Here's to a wonderful year ahead!"

"Thanks, Dad, thanks ... but don't overdo it, okay?" Marisa panted a little louder than necessary.

"That's right, Patrick. Leave a little bit of our daughter for me!" Mona embraced the girl more gently, and then looked into her eyes.

"I wish you all the best, too! You know, at fifteen –" she started a speech that Marisa knew by heart from previous years, and which her daughter now recited in a somewhat mechanical tone.

"I know, Mom! At fifteen the brain is more mature, one is intelligent enough to know how to flush the toilet, and especially, to stop getting on one's parents' nerves! One should be doing one's best at school so that one gets good grades, although I have to say 'good grades' is a relative term. Oh, yes, also very important, one should recognize that one is not automatically an adult just because one knows how to use eyeliner and lipstick." Marisa looked at them innocently. "Did I already tell you that Owen Russell, who's in eleventh grade, thinks I'm cute and has asked me if I want to be his girlfriend?" she added.

Mona looked shocked, and she realized, with some sadness, that Marisa wasn't the little girl she still thought she was.

"Well, when I was young, we didn't have boyfriends at fifteen," she began, but Marisa just laughed.

"Oh, Mom, you aren't that old! Most of the girls in my class have had a boyfriend for two years!"

"Is that so? So you think you need to catch up, so you don't remain an old maid, do you?" Patrick, amused, winked at his daughter, and then gave his wife an affectionate hug.

"Exactly!"

"Mona, what have we done wrong?" he asked, teasingly, and even Mona had to laugh.

"It's your own fault," replied Marisa, grinning, and the family looked at one another contentedly. They really had a terrific relationship with one another, and Marisa's friends were often jealous of her cool parents.

"Well, it looks as though I'll have to add an extra setting at the table from now on," Mona said.

"And speaking of table," Marisa interrupted easily and stood on tiptoe in order to see over her father's shoulders onto the table.

"Wow, raspberry mousse cake with chocolate icing! Oh, no, after this feast I'll have to starve myself for two weeks to return to my normal weight. Oh, what am I saying – three weeks, at least! But whatever!" Marisa could hardly wait to sit down at the table with her parents and let the smooth raspberry cream dissolve deliciously in her mouth.

"Mmmm ... heavenly! Dreamy! Amazing! Outrageous!" The list of praise went on for a while, until Mona, laughing, stopped her.

"That's enough, already!" she said, and exchanged a conspiratorial look with her husband. "Don't you want to know what your birthday present is?"

"Oh, Mom, nothing could compete with your chocolate-raspberry mousse cake anyway," Marisa said, but then added, "Of course, I want to know! Wait, no! Let me guess, okay? Maybe I'll figure it out."

"I'll bet you don't!" teased Patrick, helping himself to another piece of birthday cake. "Before it's all gone," he said, winking at his wife.

"Okay, so wait a minute," Marisa thought for a moment. "It won't be a book about the birds and the bees; I got that in fourth grade. A cell phone? Oh, silly me, I already have one! Hmmm ... this is not so easy ... Ten riding passes?"

Marisa's parents shook their heads.

"Then maybe a new pair of riding pants? Oh, it's not that, either? Hey, now it's getting difficult. Maybe I should have another piece of cake to give me strength."

Patrick couldn't wait any longer. "Listen up. I'll give you a clue. It's something very special, and you'll never guess what it is in a million years."

Marisa looked at her father, puzzled.

"That sounds awfully mysterious."

"Keep guessing!"

"Maybe it will help me if you tell me why I'm getting this gift for my fifteenth birthday," Marisa said, hoping to get another clue.

"Well," replied Mona. "We have noticed that you are a very special person who has given us nothing but joy. Your grades are great, you're helpful, and you never cause us worry, like so many other parents of teenage daughters. We're really proud of you, and we thought we could thank you with this present."

Marisa was embarrassed by her mother's words, but

she was also touched by her parents' sentiments. She swallowed the lump in her throat, and immediately began to cough because a cake crumb got caught in her windpipe.

Not knowing what to say in reply, she decided to keep on guessing.

At some point they'll tell me the secret, she thought to herself, having no idea what the present could be. But it had to be something really huge.

"A ... a trip, maybe?" Marisa dared to ask. After all, her parents knew that she had always dreamed of seeing the Egyptian pyramids in person.

Patrick looked at Mona.

"We could change this present into a trip, don't you think?"

However his wife just shook her head slowly.

"I think Marisa would regret it."

"Okay, you two, I give up. I'm never going to guess what it is."

"Ah, at last," said Patrick, solemnly, and then he stood up and opened the drawer of the sideboard behind his chair, and pulled out a simple envelope.

"It's inside," he said mysteriously, but before he handed it to Marisa he added, "But I want to make one thing clear. There will be no more presents this year."

Marisa grinned. "Are you sure?"

"As sure as I can be."

"Okay ... may I ... May I have my present now?"

Patrick nodded and gave her the envelope. Then he put his hand over his wife's, and both of them waited anxiously to see how Marisa would react when she saw what was inside.

"Ah ... I should eat another piece of cake first," the girl teased, seeing the expectant looks on the faces of her parents.

"Oh, no! You wanted to have it, now open it!"

"Okay! Drum roll, please ... Ta-da ... " said Marisa, and pulled out a postcard of a horse. Slowly she began to read, and her eyes grew very large. "Oh, my! No! Really?" Completely at a loss for words, she looked back and forth between her parents, who were smiling at her and nodding their heads.

"Wooooooooow! I can't believe it!" Marisa screamed, and then she held up her arms, with the card still in her hand. Suddenly she jumped up and hugged her parents, one after the other, while she kept staring at the postcard, hardly believing that she hadn't misread it.

For a very special person
A very special gift!
When you look at the picture on the other side
You'll know what we are giving you.
Take your time deciding which one,
So that you find the horse
That best suits you
Because you will spend many years of your life with it.

Happy Birthday, dear Marisa,
And stay as wonderful as you are!
We love you!

Mom & Dad

"I don't know what to say! I ... I ... wow, a horse! I would never have guessed that! Oh, I'm so happy! Thank you, thank you, thank you! You guys are the best parents in the world!"

Tears of joy ran down Marisa's cheeks, and what with crying and laughing at the same time, all she could do was squeak.

She was getting her own horse! A real horse! Egypt and the pyramids were forgotten instantly.

"It looks like the chocolate-raspberry mousse cake has lost its position of importance," Patrick responded, smiling, and took yet another piece.

Chapter 2

"It's not much farther," said Logan, and he pointed ahead. "If we turn off here, it's about another five minutes till we're at my house."

Lillian seemed astonished.

"This is the way to the old hunting lodge. I know the way, but I haven't been there in a long time. We usually ride in from the other direction.

"You know the house?" asked Logan, equally amazed. "Then you know where I live!"

"Wow, cool!" Lillian gushed. "That's great! My father took me with him a few years ago when Mr. Buchanan still lived there. He was really nice, but the house was even better. Does it still look like a big log cabin?"

"Of course! We left everything pretty much as it was. We had to put in a new floor in two rooms though."

"Terrific! And you renovated the old shed next to the house into the stable, didn't you?"

"When we took over the house, there was already a

stable, but it wasn't in very good condition," explained Logan.

"Hmmm ..."

"That's it up ahead," he said right afterward. "*Et voilà* ... Star's new home!"

"Wow, this would appeal to me, too," responded Cathy, with excitement. "The house is adorable, and the stable. Can we take a look inside?"

"You bet! Come with me." Logan jumped down from the saddle and the others followed him. One after the other, they led their horses past the open stable entrance to get a look at the inside.

"Wow, it doesn't look this big from the outside. How big are the stalls? They look really huge."

"Twelve feet by twelve feet."

"Fabulous! And you put in new windows, didn't you?"

"Yeah. Now the stable has lots of light inside. We just have to put the floor mats into the stalls tomorrow and then everything's finished. There's even a sack of feed and some hay. So everything is set for Star to move in next week ... and Rondo, too, of course, if you want," added Logan, looking at his girlfriend. He put his arm around her shoulder.

Even though Beth was still attached to Mercy Ranch, she knew as soon as she saw this idyllic horse paradise that Rondo would feel at home here. Logan wouldn't have to ask her twice if she wanted to put her Arabian here with Star.

"I'm overwhelmed," said Beth, and leaned against Logan. "Rondo will absolutely move in!"

Logan smiled as he ushered his friends out back.

"I thought you'd like it here. And in the back meadow,

over there," he pointed, "we've already fenced in a paddock. It's so large that it'll be easy to divide it if we need to. And during the winter, the horses can be in this small paddock we made behind the stable."

"Small?" grinned Kevin. "Some horses would be more than happy with this much space. Really Logan, I'm amazed! If Ricki ever throws me out of the Sulai stable, I hope you'll still have a stall for Sharazan," he joked, but Ricki didn't think it was funny. Maybe because of the dream.

"I'll only throw you out if you give me a reason to," she responded and then looked around abruptly when she heard a door closing.

"Hello! So my ears weren't deceiving me! I suddenly had the feeling that a whole battalion of horse soldiers had arrived." Angela Bendix had come out of the house and was now admiring the horses.

"Your horses are all so beautiful ... My goodness, he's so sweet!" Logan's mother stopped in front of old Jonah; the old horse had made a very magical impression on her. "That would be mine!" she said spontaneously. "I love big horses, but unfortunately, I can't ride."

Hal recognized a look of regret in her eyes.

"Oh, nonsense, anyone can ride Jonah. He's as gentle as a lamb," he said, gesturing invitingly at Logan's mother. "Would you like to ride him? I don't think the old boy would mind."

Angela Bendix laughed.

"No, I'd rather not. He's so big I'd be afraid of the height up there."

"Oh, come on, Mom, don't be a coward," laughed Logan.

"Maybe next time," she tried to talk herself out of it.

"But that's a promise, Mrs. Bendix, isn't it?" Hal grinned.

"Yes ... yes."

"And we all heard it!"

"Oh boy, then I guess I must keep it the next time you come."

"Yup!"

"Well, all right, but in that case, better give me some time before your next visit so I can prepare myself physically and mentally," she pleaded.

"Hey, Mom, this is Beth and her horse, Rondo. You know ..."

Angela held out her hand amicably to her son's girlfriend.

"I'm happy to finally meet you, Beth. Logan has told us so much about you. Have you looked around the stable yet, and do you think Rondo would like it here?"

Beth shook the pleasant woman's hand.

"The stable is absolutely fabulous! If it's okay, I'd very much like to board Rondo here!"

"Of course it's okay." Angela Bendix nodded to Beth. She was happy that Logan had such a nice girlfriend and that he had found so many new friends in the young riders. And she was delighted that the pleasant girl wanted to board her horse with Star.

Logan's mother was sure that with Beth's help her son wouldn't revert to his former wild lifestyle. Before Logan and his family moved here from New York City, Logan had hung out with a bad crowd and had gotten in trouble for vandalism, which cost his family quite a lot in damages and embarrassment. But after that awful time, he had promised his mother that he would never do anything to hurt his family again, and it seemed as though he was being true to his word.

While the others talked, Cheryl sighed and leaned against Sheila pensively. "Do you think it's expensive to build a stable like this?"

Lillian pushed out her lower lip.

"Well, I think it wasn't cheap. It always depends on whether you have to build a whole new building or if you already have something that you can add on to or renovate."

Cheryl took a deep breath.

"At the moment, I should just be happy that I have Sheila and she's at Carlotta's ranch, where I can always take care of her and ride her whenever I want. That's great too, isn't it? Not everyone can have their own stables or, for that matter, their own horses. I guess I'll never have one ..."

"Why don't you just wait and see," replied Lillian. "At the very least, when you're grown up and earning your own money, you can think it over and decide whether you want to buy one or not."

"That's true. But whether or not Sheila will still be there when I'm able to afford my own horse is questionable," Cheryl responded with a sad glance at the black-and white mare.

"There are other horses," said Lillian, after hesitating a bit, but she knew that it wasn't a good answer.

"But not one of them is like Sheila. She's one of a kind!"

***

When the riders arrived back at Mercy Ranch, they found a very strange scene.

From a distance they had seen the vet's SUV parked out front and wondered what had happened.

"Good grief, Carlotta, what's wrong?" asked Beth, frightened, as she dismounted from Rondo and led him into the stable corridor. There she saw Kieran standing with Jam, trying to calm him down as Dr. Hofer, the vet, slowly sewed one stitch after another in an attempt to patch up a rather large wound in the horse's chest.

Carlotta stood beside him and handed him thread and cotton pads as he asked for them. Keeping her focus on Jam and the vet, she recounted the accident.

"Jam was galloping across the paddock and he stumbled, crashing right into the paddock fence poles, where they're thinner than in the rest of the fence. One of the poles split and tore a hole in his chest. Thank heavens Kieran was already here; he was able to keep the horse quiet while I called Dr. Hofer."

The vet reached out his hand to Carlotta. "Please, another cotton pad ... and another one. This is pretty bad, but we're going to fix him up. Don't worry, Carlotta! Despite everything, it looks worse than it is," the vet said and reached out his hand again. "Please, pass me the scalpel again. I have to smooth out the edge of the wound so I can sew him up."

Beth had only glanced at the wound as she walked past, but what she saw was enough to turn her stomach.

She brought Rondo quickly into his stall, unsaddled him, and spoke quietly to him to calm him. When the animal saw his stable mate's blood, he got very agitated.

"You probably should have left him outside," reacted Carlotta, with a side-glance at the Arabian. "Horses are very sensitive about this."

Beth nodded.

"Should I take him back outside?" she asked.

"No, leave him in his stall now," answered Dr. Hofer, not taking his eyes off of the wound. "If you lead your horse past us again, Jam will get even more upset, and then I'll have a problem. But you can go outside and tell your friends what's going on. We don't want them bringing in their horses too."

"Okay, I'll do that." Beth left Rondo's stall and ran outside without looking at Jam's chest again. She wondered how Kieran and Carlotta could stand it.

Just in time, she was able to stop Logan, Cheryl, and Hal, who were standing outside the door to the stable.

"Hey, guys, don't go any farther. Jam is being stitched up in the stable. You're supposed to leave the horses outside until Dr. Hofer is finished," she called to her friends.

"What?"

"Oh, my goodness, what happened?"

"Come on, tell us!"

So Beth filled them in.

* * *

Ricki, Lillian, Cathy, and Kevin had arrived back home in the meantime, and they stood at the edge of the paddock watching their horses rolling around in the grass after the long ride.

"That must feel good," said Kevin, peacefully.

"You can do it, too," giggled Cathy. "However, your mother may not be too pleased about the grass stains all over your clothes."

"Ha, ha! Well, I'm not a horse, am I?"

"There was a film called *They Called Him Horse,* or something like that," responded Lillian.

"Well, I didn't play the main character in that film, if that's what you're getting at."

"No, you're more like those two old guys from the *Muppet Show*!" Ricki burst out.

"Say, didn't you three enjoy the ride? Or did you just get too much sun?" Kevin looked annoyed. "Why are women always so mean?"

The three girls grinned at each other.

"And you're all in agreement, once again. Terrific!" Kevin snorted in artificial anger. "Three against one, that's typical! Just wait, Ricki, maybe I'll move to Logan's with Sharazan voluntarily." Now Kevin chuckled, but Ricki's face fell.

"That wasn't funny!" She turned away quickly and ran across the field to the stable.

"Now what did I say?" asked Kevin, perplexed by Ricki's reaction.

"Oh, it's probably connected to the dream she had last night, the one where you broke up with her," Lillian informed him. "But don't tell her I told you. She'd kill me!"

"Hah! Now I have you," teased Kevin, but he turned serious right away. "But that's crazy! I would never do that. I care about her too much!"

"Then tell her that. Maybe then she'll calm down," suggested Cathy, and Kevin nodded.

"Yeah, it's probably the best thing to do. Give me ten minutes, then you can follow me," he said, sounding like an inspector in a detective story. Then he ran after Ricki, and caught up with her before she reached the stable.

Lillian and Cathy watched the meeting, and when Kevin wrapped his arms around his girlfriend, the girls winked at each other.

"It looks like everything's back to normal."

After one more look at the horses, now grazing peacefully on the paddock, the two of them walked back to the stable to clean and put away their riding gear. They knew if they didn't they'd never hear the end of it from Jake, who hated when things weren't where they belonged.

* * *

Late in the afternoon the friends were hanging out in Ricki's room when suddenly she remembered something, and pulled a wrinkled piece of paper from her jeans pocket.

"Did you guys get this invitation from the riding club too?" she asked, holding up the paper.

"What invitation?" asked Lillian.

"Listen to this. I'll read it to you."

To members of the Avalon Riding Academy, as well as all horse lovers in the area.

Summer is almost here, and just as the temperature is rising, so too is our desire to be with horses – riding, participating in games, having fun – in short, enjoying everything having to do with our beloved four-legged friends.

Of course, our official tournament season is starting as well, and we hope that many of you will participate again this year. However, there are also many riders among us who prefer casual riding to tournament riding and jumping. So this year, we have come up with something special just for you!

In the next eight weeks we will hold a Fun and Games Festival for members and nonmembers who aren't so keen on precision events. The festival will feature various fun riding games, with points awarded to the participants, who will receive ribbons for their placement, just as in our regular tournaments.

Doesn't that sound like fun? Tell us what you think. We'd love to hear your ideas and get your feedback. By the way, we are open to any suggestions for riding games and would appreciate receiving your suggestions by the end of the month.

Please register within the allotted time period if you are interested in participating in our Fun and Games Festival. If we don't receive enough registrations, we will be forced to cancel the event. However, it is our hope that the festival will be such a hit that it can become an annual event.

And as for our members who don't ride, we still need your help to make the day a huge success. We're looking for volunteers to donate picnic food, or help out in a variety of other ways.

We look forward to receiving your registration and hope that all of our expectations for a fun day with happy riders and horses will be fulfilled.

Sincerely,
Avalon Riding Academy
Nick Rizzo, board chairman and club manager

"Well, what do you all think of that?" asked Ricki as soon as she finished reading.

"Hey, that really sounds like fun, although I have to ask myself who wrote that thing. It couldn't have been Rizzo. That old grump would never have used that friendly tone!" responded Lillian.

"I don't mind Rizzo," said Cathy, after thinking it over quickly. "If Carlotta doesn't have any objections, I'd like to take part in it with Rashid."

"I'm sure that won't be a problem." Kevin nodded to Cathy. "Carlotta is always in favor of things like that. She'll be more likely to regret that she isn't fit enough to take part in it."

"You might be right about that. I think I'll register, too," said Ricki, her eyes glowing. "I'm just not suited for normal riding and jumping tournaments anymore, because all I do is trail ride with Diablo, but I think we'd be able to play a few games."

"Absolutely! So, we're all going to enter, okay?" Cathy was very excited.

"Yes!"

"We could ask the others at Mercy Ranch tomorrow," Kevin suggested. "I think Beth and Logan will love the idea, and I'm sure some of the others will, too."

"Hah! Whether Logan will be happy about seeing Rizzo again is another matter altogether." Lillian reminded them that the chairman of the riding club had made the boy's life miserable after Logan moved to town. Without any justification, Rizzo had told Logan to leave with his horse and never come back.

"Did he ever apologize to Logan?" Cathy wanted to know.

"I don't think so."

"Well, let's ask him anyway. It would be great if all of us could take part, wouldn't it?"

Ricki nodded. "And it would be something completely different than just riding through the countryside, as much as I love doing that."

"That's true. Oh, you know what? I'm going to ask

Josh, too. Maybe a few others from the Western ranch would come. That would really be fun!" said Lillian, whose boyfriend was a devoted Western-style rider.

"Do you think they got a note, too?"

"I have no idea, but I didn't get one," said Kevin.

"Ricki, when did you get yours?"

"It was in the mailbox today."

Lillian looked at her watch and got up.

"People, as much as I hate to leave, I have to get home. We have a Spanish test tomorrow and I have to review all the grammar again, or I'm going to do really badly."

Cathy and Kevin stood up, too.

"Time to say good-bye," Kevin began singing. "I have to study, too."

"Why?" asked Ricki, puzzled.

"Did you forget? We have a math test in two days."

Ricki fell back on her chair.

"Oh, no! That's in two days? Uh ... Cathy, you have to explain that stuff to me again, or I'm done for."

Cathy, the math genius, grinned broadly.

"Right now or tomorrow?" she asked.

"Never do right now what you can put off till the day after tomorrow!" answered Ricki, ever the procrastinator when it came to schoolwork. "Tomorrow night, okay? That way I hope I can still remember thirty percent of your explanations the next day."

"If you could retain that much, you'd be really good!" teased Cathy and ducked to avoid the pillow Ricki threw at her.

* * *

It took Marisa at least half an hour to calm down and make

sure that her parents' gift wasn't just a joke, and then she began to think about what her dream horse would look like.

Friesian and Black Forest Shire horses were always high on her list, followed by Arabians, Palominos, and Paints. Actually, she loved all horses, no matter what their breed. Before it had been easy to say, "If I could choose a horse, it would be a Friesian" or whatever, but now that she actually could choose, it was much more difficult.

Her own horse ... with no warning, out of the blue ... she was so lucky!

The card had said that she should take her time choosing the right horse, and Marisa knew that it was the right thing to do. But for someone who had wished for her own horse her whole life, now that she had the opportunity, it seemed as if every minute without a horse was a waste.

Marisa took a deep breath and began to think.

Sometimes, through various members of the riding club, she knew when someone was selling a horse, but she hadn't heard anything recently.

Maybe I should just look in the newspaper first and see what's being offered, the girl thought, and got up to get the daily paper from the living room.

Back in her room, she spread out the paper on her bed and then sat down cross-legged in front of it and looked for the ads offering animals for sale.

When she found the advertising section, she read aloud, "Alpacas ... angora rabbits ... Afghan hound ..."

"If I were spinning yarn, I'd be thrilled!" Marisa murmured to herself, before reading on.

"German shepherd mix ... Pekinese ... Siamese cats ... kittens ... miniature bunnies ... guinea pigs ..."

"Oh, there are always horses in here, but just not today. I don't believe it!" she said, resigned, and was about to close the paper when she spied two ads from horse dealers.

Marisa thought it over. Horse dealers have a huge selection of horses, but often you didn't find out much about the animals – where they were from, how they grew up, how they had been treated – and Marisa had heard that there were bad horse dealers who knew precisely how to cover up various defects in their horses.

"So not a horse dealer," Marisa decided for herself. She hoped that in the next few days a few private people would put ads in the paper to sell a horse, and until then she would just have to be patient.

"A few days aren't going to make any difference now," she tried to tell herself, but this kind of reasoning didn't seem to work. Her parents wanted to give her a horse, and she wanted to have one as soon as possible.

Well, but not just any horse.

Marisa bunched up the newspaper and threw it in the corner. Then she lay down on her bed, folded her arms under her head, and stared at the ceiling.

She wondered what her girlfriends were going to say.

Probably nothing. Marisa answered her own question. After all, not a single one of them was a riding fan.

Then she remembered her cousin Beth, with whom she hadn't been in contact for quite a while. Beth had her own horse, so it was possible that she would know about someone selling a horse.

Maybe she should just call her? They had always gotten along well and, in retrospect, Marisa really didn't know why they had lost contact.

Determined, she got up and ran right into the kitchen, where her mother was standing at the stove.

"Hey, Mom, do you have Beth's phone number?"

Mona smiled at her daughter. "Beth who?"

"Beth! The daughter of your sister? My cousin? Your niece! Dad's niece-in-law!"

"Niece-in-law? Is there even such a thing?"

"I have no idea. But the main thing is, what is her phone number?"

Mona thought it over. "Wait a minute, they moved a few months ago." Mona walked to the living room and pulled out one of the drawers of the sideboard. She rummaged around inside, picked up a bunch of papers, put them back, and then rummaged some more.

"I could have sworn I put my address book in here," she said, looking bewildered.

"Don't tell me you can't find it!"

"It seems like it."

Suddenly there was a loud hissing noise coming from the kitchen.

"Heavens! My gravy is boiling over!" Mona ran back to the kitchen. "I'll look for the number later, okay, sweetie? The address book has to be somewhere. I have to see if I can save this gravy right now."

"Darn it! Oh well, then I can't do anything about it now." Disappointed, Marisa left.

Now I have some real news to tell, and no one to tell it to, she thought. *Life just isn't fair!* Then she began to laugh at her own logic and disappeared into her room to check horse sales online.

* * *

Late in the evening, a small lamp still lit the corridor of the Mercy Ranch stable, its ray of light faint enough to keep from disturbing the horses.

Carlotta had decided to check on her patient, Jam. The animal had seemed to be in shock for a long time after she brought him back to his stall following Dr. Hofer's excellent care.

"Good evening, you poor boy. How are you doing?" she asked softly, her voice heavy with compassion. "Are you in pain? Of course you are, aren't you? Unfortunately, you just have to get through this, my boy! Why did you have to gallop so fast in the paddock?" Carlotta stretched her hand over the top of the stall's half door and could just manage to stroke Jam's soft, velvety nostrils.

The animal standing in front of her was completely apathetic; he didn't seem to know that she was even there.

"I'm going to leave you in peace. Sleep well, young man! I'll check on you tomorrow morning. Get better fast, you hear me?" Carlotta nodded to him and then went from box to box, as she did every evening, to say good night to each of her horses.

She stayed a little longer with Sheila.

Pensively, she looked at the beautiful mare, who came right over to Carlotta, full of trust, and snorted in her hair.

"Oh, if you knew what I did today," the ranch owner said softly, feeling a lump in her throat. "Soon you may be going to a new home, Sheila, but I hope you know that it isn't easy for me to give you up. I promise that I'll find a good one for you. No, a very good one, where you'll be happy and the people will love you!" Suddenly, Carlotta's eyes welled up with tears. "Forgive me, Sheila, but I have to do it."

With a heavy heart, she turned off the light and went back into her house.

Restlessly, she paced from one room to the next, and made a cup of coffee even though she knew it would keep her up half the night. She figured she wouldn't be able to sleep anyway. First Jam's accident, which really upset her, and then Sheila ... oh, yes, and then there was her proposal for a small riding hall, which she had planned to the last detail but which now would probably never happen. The construction was going to be a lot more expensive than they had originally estimated, meaning she would have to have regular summer guests for the next two years in order to pay for it.

Too bad, thought Carlotta. *But the hall will just have to wait a little longer. That doesn't mean it will never happen. Someday I'll manage to get it done!* What really bothered her was that the architect had miscalculated so badly but, thank heaven, it had been discovered before she had begun any construction.

Carlotta sighed deeply. At the moment, life wasn't exactly easy, but she knew from experience that there was always a silver lining. Since she was confident in her decision-making, knowing that even if she spent the whole night thinking about it she wouldn't change her mind, she decided to go to bed. She would go to sleep at some point and, in the morning ... yes, tomorrow morning would be a new day and she would make the best of it.

Chapter 3

The following morning Logan called Beth fairly early.

"Hey, I won't be coming to the ranch until about noon today. My father and I want to cut the stall mats to the right size and put them down, and that's going to take a while. But if we get done with them today, then we could move the horses in tomorrow."

"That sounds great! Tomorrow would be perfect. School will be over pretty early so we'll have enough time to do it," answered Beth, her heart beating loudly.

"That's what I thought." Logan paused briefly. "Have I told you today that I'm crazy about you?" he asked after they made their plans, and Beth closed her eyes happily.

"No, you haven't! But even if you had, I still love to hear you say it."

Logan smiled, even though Beth couldn't see him.

"Okay, then I'll see you later. So long."

"Okay, bye!" Beth put the receiver down slowly. Her time at Mercy Ranch was almost over. She had to say good-bye to

Carlotta, who had offered Rondo and Star stalls when Beth and Logan had had problems finding a stable.

I think it would be nice to take Carlotta a little gift today to say thank you, Beth thought, and she knew instantly what she wanted to give her.

She ran into her room and took a large crystal block down from her shelf. In it was a beautiful mare with her foal, engraved by laser. On one hand, it was hard for Beth to give up this decorative piece she loved. She had saved for months, doing all sorts of work, to buy it. But on the other hand dear Carlotta, with her generosity and warmth, deserved a special present, and that made it possible for Beth to part with it.

One last time Beth looked closely at the glass, and then searched through a chest where she kept all sorts of things including pieces of gift-wrapping. She found some paper with rainbows and clouds on it, which reminded her of the peacefulness of the ranch, and took it out.

"Oh, it's a little wrinkled," she mumbled to herself, but after she had stretched the paper across the edge of the table a few times, it seemed good enough for her to wrap the crystal in, after she first wrapped it in newspaper for protection. Then she wrote a little card, which she cut out of a postcard, and attached it to the package.

Dear Carlotta, thank you for everything! Beth and Logan

Satisfied, she nodded and then looked at her alarm clock. It was just 9 a.m. By the time she reached the ranch on her bike it would be 10, and that was the perfect time. She would probably find Carlotta having her second cup of coffee. Beth changed into her riding clothes and started off.

When she turned in to Mercy Ranch shortly before 10 o'clock, the first thing she saw was Cheryl's bike, which was leaning against the house as usual, since there was no bike stand.

Beth was glad. She liked Cheryl and had become good friends with her.

"Hello, is anyone here?" called Beth as she ran into the stable. When she saw Cheryl and Carlotta standing in front of Jam's box with serious expressions on their faces, she slowed down abruptly and lowered her voice.

"Hey," she said quietly, "how's Jam doing?"

Carlotta shook her head slowly.

"Not very well, it seems. I'll be glad when Dr. Hofer comes by and checks him again."

"Oh," said Beth, somberly.

Jam really looked miserable. His downcast head was stretched toward one corner of his stall and he didn't react to Carlotta's words of comfort or to the fact that Beth had just joined them. Normally he was very curious, the first one to stick his head up over the edge of his stall to see who was coming and going in the stable. In addition, he didn't seem to have eaten anything. The hay in the rack and the power feed in his trough were untouched, and Beth had the feeling that Jam's only wish was to be left alone.

Carlotta turned away.

"Would you like some tea?" she asked, a forced smile on her lips.

"Tea would be great!" replied Cheryl, and Beth nodded.

"Then come on. We can't do anything here anyway."

While Carlotta boiled water for the tea in the kitchen, Cheryl grabbed a newspaper that had been lying on the

table and began to skim it, and Beth took out her present
and put it at Carlotta's place without anyone noticing.

"Do you know exactly when you're going to move
Rondo and Star?" asked Carlotta casually.

"Logan said if they lay the stall mats today, we could
move the horses in tomorrow."

"Ah. Tomorrow. So soon? Heavens, how time flies.
It feels as though you just arrived last week." Carlotta
brought a teapot filled with the hot tea over to the girls.

"Make a little space," she said to Cheryl, who had
spread out the newspaper across the table.

Cheryl was just about to fold the newspaper when she
noticed the ads for animal sales.

"They're selling all kinds of animals. Fancy fish,
mountain goats, a lizard – Carlotta, could you use a lizard?"
And while she was laughing at the thought of a lizard living
in the horse stalls at Mercy Ranch, she suddenly jerked her
head.

"Someone's selling a 'Black Forest Shire mare, very
affectionate, ideal character, easy to load onto trailers, good
with blacksmiths, one hundred percent reliable,'" Cheryl
sighed. "That could be Sheila. I always ask myself why
horses like that are sold. I mean, people should be glad they
have a horse like that. So why do they sell them?"

Carlotta was stunned. She had completely forgotten that her
ad would be in the Saturday paper. Oh, why did she have to
leave yesterday's newspaper lying around in the kitchen? Now
Cheryl had found Sheila's ad, and Carlotta had intended to tell
the girl gently that she was going to sell the horse.

"Sometimes you have to do things that you don't want
to do," she said, as she sat down awkwardly and looked

at Cheryl. "And sometimes outside forces make you to do something you don't want to do."

"I still don't understand it."

"Look, how would you react if I sold Sheila?" Carlotta forced herself to ask.

"You would NEVER do that! And if you did ... then ... then I think it would be because of the ranch somehow."

Carlotta nodded.

"See. And that would be a legitimate reason. But aside from that, do you remember that I once said that I wanted to find good homes for some of our horses, so that here at Mercy Ranch there would always be space for real emergencies?"

"Yeah, of course. That makes sense."

"Okay, Cheryl, then you understand that these ads aren't always written by mean people who just want to get rid of their horses?"

The girl nodded hesitantly.

"Yeah, but I would never sell my horse. Never!" she said stubbornly. "Oh, thanks for the tea."

"Carlotta, I want to –" began Beth, after a short pause in the conversation, thinking that the subject was over, but Carlotta interrupted her.

"Just a minute, Beth, please ... Cheryl, I wanted to tell you this another way, but ... did you read the telephone number under the ad for the mare?"

"No." The girl grinned. "Do you want to get a friend for Sheila? Just a minute, let me look." Quickly, the girl unfolded the newspaper. "Where was that? ... Oh, here! The number is –" Before she had even spoken the rest of the numbers, she turned pale. "That's ... that's your number!"

Carlotta nodded, and gradually Cheryl began to understand.

"Sheila? You're not serious, are you? You want to sell Sheila? But you can't do that! She ... I ... Please, Carlotta, tell me this isn't true!" Cheryl's lower lip began to quiver, as she hoped Carlotta would give the answer she wanted to hear, but the older woman remained silent and kept her gaze on Cheryl.

Sobbing, the girl jumped up from the chair and ran outside, where she grabbed her bike and raced from the yard in deep despair. It wasn't possible for Cheryl to stay there a minute longer, and she certainly couldn't go to Sheila. The worst thing she could have imagined had happened. Sheila was going to be sold! Her Sheila! The horse that meant so much to her. She would probably never see her again, never again be able to stroke her soft coat, never again would she gaze into her wonderful, wise eyes ... and her heart would never stop aching.

"Carlotta, how could you do this to me?" She sobbed against the bright shining sun, as the tears began to flow.

* * *

Shocked, Beth looked at Carlotta, who was trying to regain her composure.

"Carlotta ... I ..." began Beth, but then she was silent.

The gift was completely forgotten in the wake of what Carlotta and Cheryl were now feeling.

Almost timidly, Beth got up and quietly went outside. She sensed that Carlotta wanted to be alone right now.

Her head bowed in sadness, Beth slipped into the stable and went to Rondo's stall, as she thought of Cheryl.

She hugged her horse's neck tightly.

"I know exactly how she feels!" she whispered to him.

"I will never forget how I felt when Dad sold you! Never! I feel so sorry for Cheryl."

* * *

Carlotta sat with her head in her hands, just as Beth had left her. She was so saddened by what her decision had done to Cheryl. She liked Cheryl very much, and she certainly had never wanted to hurt her.

"You should have found another way to do it, Carlotta Mancini," she accused herself. "You should have found a way to tell her more gently!" But she realized that Cheryl's reaction would have been the same no matter how or when she broke the news to her.

She sighed deeply and leaned back in her chair, and then caught sight of the pretty gift-wrapped present, which she hadn't noticed before.

Who had put it here?

It didn't take long for the answer to occur to her. She reached across the table for the gift, and was amazed at how heavy it was. Very carefully she unwrapped the present.

Incredulous, she stared at the gorgeous crystal decoration. Then she noticed the card which lay on the table beside the wrapping paper.

After she'd read the message, her eyes filled with tears; she was so moved. That simple sentence *"Thanks for everything!"* went directly to her heart, and was enough to make her completely lose her composure. Cheryl would never write these words to her. She wouldn't thank her for making her so unhappy.

Carlotta wiped her eyes and got up to look for Beth. However, when she finally entered the stable, she noticed that the girl had already left to go riding with Rondo.

* * *

With much laughter, Ricki, Lillian, Cathy, and Kevin carried four old chairs, two buckets of water, and twenty plastic poles out to the paddock.

"If you keep on like this all the water will spill out before we even get there," giggled Ricki, as she watched Kevin trying desperately to lose as little water as possible.

"Hey, these things are heavy! My arms are getting longer by the minute!" Panting, the boy put down his load for a moment to catch his breath.

"Hey, we forgot the Ping-Pong balls and the spoons," remarked Lillian.

"And we need apples, too. And the paper streamers," added Ricki. "But we couldn't have carried everything in one load anyway. Too bad we don't have a few more bales of straw."

"Just a minute! If you're thinking of asking me to carry bales of straw the whole way, then I'm suddenly going to remember an appointment that I can't miss. Could you please explain to me why I have to carry these enormous buckets of water?" asked Kevin rubbing his wrists and groaning.

"I'll tell you later, when everything's ready."

"I can hardly wait."

"Don't complain! After all, you were very enthusiastic about practicing a few riding games in order to see how our horses do before we register for the Fun and Games Festival." Ricki picked up the plastic poles again and marched off.

"I'm sure that riding games are terrific, but after all this work my arms hurt so much I probably won't even be able to heave the saddle onto Sharazan's back." Kevin sighed loudly and then, complaining even louder, he carried his heavy load farther. The path from the stable to the paddock had never seemed so long to him before.

* * *

"Okay, listen up," announced Ricki after about an hour, when the games were prepared and the four friends were lined up on the horses at the entrance to the paddock.

"I suggest that we try the slalom race first. We need to see if we put the poles in at the right intervals or we should put them farther apart."

"Want me to try a gallop first?" asked Kevin, and Lillian nodded.

"Yeah, go ahead. I can't wait to see if you can do it."

Kevin grinned confidently.

"Piece of cake!" he replied, before stopping Sharazan a few yards from one of the two rows that had ten poles each.

"Then go," called Ricki. "But remember, you can't knock down any poles and you can't leave any out, or you'll be disqualified."

"Okay, Sharazan, here we go!" Kevin concentrated and then he gave his roan the sign to start galloping and tried to steer him, without slowing down, in a zigzag course through the poles. However, after his horse hit three poles he just gave up and galloped straight ahead.

"Noooo! It's impossible!" Kevin came back to the girls, laughing. "I would never have thought it could be so hard."

"Yeah, yeah, 'piece of cake'! Ha, ha! Men!" teased Cathy. But Kevin just replied, "Okay, show me how you can do it better, woman! Come on! You have to do better than three poles!"

Cathy galloped off, but Rashid had enough after only one turn and just stood still as his rider tried to navigate him around the second pole.

"Wow, what a catastrophe!" she called out.

Lillian laughed heartily. "Now let me try. Out of my way!"

Holli was good. With Lillian's help, he made it around six poles with almost no problem. However, at the seventh pole, she bumped into it with her stirrup and knocked it down.

Cathy ran over immediately and put the pole back in place.

"Hey, and I always thought Holli wasn't flexible because he's so gigantic!" said Kevin with admiration.

"I have to admit that I've already done this with him before. Josh gave me a few tips." Lillian winked at Ricki. "Now you! Show us what Diablo can do!"

"Maybe I should just run through the poles without him," laughed the girl, and then she started Diablo in a gallop, but made only four out of the ten poles.

She came back to the starting position a little disappointed.

"Well, if we can't do this, then we can't even think about registering for the tournament. This is one of the simplest games, one that even a child can do on a pony."

"Ponies are smaller and can maneuver more easily," objected Cathy, but Ricki shook her head.

"That's true, but we put the poles very far apart, so our horses shouldn't have a problem with this."

"We just can't do it!" was the decision Kevin finally came to after many unsuccessful tries.

"Oh, come on! We have a lot of time until the tournament. We'll just practice this every day."

Cathy groaned.

"Have I mentioned lately how much I love riding to Echo Lake?"

"No, no! We're not going riding until each of us can go through this slalom without a mistake!" shouted Ricki, now totally serious.

Kevin tapped his forehead. "Sharazan wants me to tell you that you're crazy," he grinned.

"That's nothing new," Ricki winked in reply, and then she pointed to all the other stuff the kids had carried out to the paddock. "Do you guys feel like trying something different?"

"Definitely, but let's make it something easier," pleaded Cathy, so Ricki distributed a few paper streamers.

"This isn't so hard. You have to ride in pairs, holding a stretched out streamer between you. You have to ride various figures next to each other with one hand, without letting the paper streamer rip. Maybe we should try just riding around the paddock first, and then maybe in circles, or whatever."

"Cathy, you ride next to me," ordered Lillian, before unrolling the streamer and giving her girlfriend the other end.

Ricki mounted her horse and then gave Kevin the other end of the thin paper streamer.

"Okay, we're ready, too. First, just walk around. Trotting and galloping will come later."

Rashid and Holli started off. It wasn't a problem for the two girls to walk in circles or curves, but as soon as they increased their speed it was very different.

"Oops," said Lillian as her hand made a tiny movement that ripped the thin strip of paper immediately.

"We won!" grinned Kevin.

"That was only a test ride," Cathy defended the paper streamer misfortune. She unrolled a new streamer, and then she and Lillian rode across the paddock.

At the first test gallop, Ricki and Kevin were out of the race after the third lap because Sharazan pushed past Diablo about a horse's length.

"We have to make sure that we ride exactly next to each other, or this won't work."

"If we can't manage riding straight ahead, how are we going to do it galloping in a circle with one hand?" Kevin asked himself. "I'll tell you one thing, if Josh and his Western group participate in this Fun and Games Festival, we're all going to look stupid and we won't have a chance of winning anything. They're spectacular at riding with one hand."

"We have no idea if these games that we're practicing are going to be part of the tournament," Cathy said. "Maybe they've thought of completely different ones."

"But if we can do this stuff, then we could send these suggestions to Rizzo, and hope that they'll use our ideas. Then maybe we wouldn't look so bad after all!" replied Lillian.

"Well, I'll tell you one thing," Kevin looked at the others. "If I don't make a major improvement in two weeks, I'm not going to register for the games tournament."

Ricki laughed at him.

"Coward! That's exactly the fun of it: that it doesn't always turn out the way it should. It's a tournament for F-U-N!!! Get it? Fun!"

"Yeah, I know! But then I ask myself why I should put myself through all this stress."

"Stress? Where?"

"I really enjoy this!"

"And the whole thing makes me laugh myself silly!"

The three girls looked at each other and started to laugh.

"Oh, man, I have never seen girls as single-minded as you three are."

"See! We always prove the statistics wrong."

"What? Is there a statistic about this?"

"Hey, are you all turning into mathematicians, or can we keep going?" asked Lillian, and then added, after she had looked into the plastic bag lying on the ground, "By the way, the paper streamers are all gone."

"Already? They went really fast. It doesn't matter, I have more in the house." Ricki looked at the chairs. "We could play an interesting water game." She turned to Kevin. "You're going to love this – and afterwards you'll be soaking wet!" She laughed so loudly that Diablo, frightened by the noise, skittered sideways.

"Oh no, what did I do to deserve this?" groaned Kevin, but then he accepted his fate. "Okay, tell me what brand of torture you've picked out for me next!"

* * *

Marisa reread the Saturday paper closely, hoping that she had missed an ad for a horse, but unfortunately she had not.

"There's really nothing in here!" she said dejectedly. "Besides the stupid dealers!"

"Don't worry about it, I'm sure the right horse is just waiting for you," responded Mona sympathetically. "By the way, I found the address book. I put it in another drawer. If you'd like, you could call Beth now. I think she'd really be glad to hear from you after such a long time."

Marisa's face lit up.

"That's great news! Of course, not as good as an ad for a horse, but still." She grinned and grabbed the cordless phone. "Where did you say the number is?"

Mona went to the kitchen and came right back with a little slip of paper.

"Oh, great! Thanks, Mom." Marisa took off.

Actually, Marisa felt a little funny calling Beth, because they hadn't had any contact for so long. On the other hand, she couldn't wait to tell her cousin that soon she would be a proud horse owner, too. That is, if someone was selling a horse that suited her.

At the moment, it doesn't look like it, thought Marisa, as she dialed the number and then nervously waited for someone to pick up the phone.

"Pendleton residence," Marisa's aunt answered after several rings.

"Oh, hi, Aunt Nancy! This is Marisa."

"Marisa? Hello! How are you? We haven't heard from you Swintons for quite some time. How are your parents? Is everything okay?" Nancy Pendleton was very glad to hear from her niece.

The girl laughed.

"You all haven't called us either! Mom and Dad are fine and so am I."

"It was your birthday yesterday, wasn't it? Best wishes, belatedly! I'm sorry I forgot all about it."

"Thanks, that's okay. Can I speak to Beth? It's really important."

51

"Not at the moment, I'm afraid. She's out riding and I'm not sure when she'll be back."

"Oh, that's too bad."

"Would you like her cell phone number?"

"That would be great! Wait a second, I have to get something to write on ... Okay, go ahead." Marisa wrote down the number that her aunt dictated.

"Thanks a lot, Aunt Nancy! Mom told me to tell you hello from her. She lost your new address, but I think she'll be calling you soon. At least that's what she said a while ago."

"Great! Then please tell your parents I said hello, too. If you do reach Beth on her cell, would you please tell her that she has to be home by eight? Will you do that for me?"

"Of course, I'll do that. Bye!" Marisa bit her lip to keep from laughing, and hoped she wouldn't forget what she was asked to do.

Chapter 4

Marisa reached Beth on her cell phone just as she was closing the paddock gate after bringing Rondo out to the meadow.

"Hi, cuz, I'm so glad to hear from you! What's up?" Beth was really excited. She liked her cousin very much. "What? You got an I.O.U. for a horse for your birthday? That's amazing! Incredible! Fabulous! Oh, and happy birthday, too!" Both Beth and Marisa laughed. Then the soon-to-be horse owner told her cousin about her problem.

"Usually there are tons of offers for horses in the paper, but now there are none at all. Zero. Do you know how frustrating that is?" complained Marisa. Beth completely understood how she felt.

"Well, they don't know that you're looking for a horse," she tried to joke, but Marisa turned serious.

"Hey, you know so many people who ride. Isn't there someone you know who's selling a horse? Naturally I'm going to look at several different animals before I make a decision, but first I have to have some animals to look at."

Beth thought it over.

"No, at the moment ... wait a minute!" All of a sudden she remembered Carlotta. "Listen. I have Rondo boarded at Mercy Ranch right now – well, actually, he's moving to another stable tomorrow, but that doesn't matter. There's a really sweet Black Forest Shire mare that's for sale. She's very pretty, gentle, super to ride and not very old, I think. I'm sure you'd like Sheila."

Inwardly, Beth pleaded with Cheryl to forgive her. She knew her girlfriend hoped that no buyer would be found for Sheila for a long, long time. On the other hand, if the animal was in Marisa's care, then she would be one hundred percent certain that Shelia would be happy and well looked after. Marisa was wonderful with horses.

"What? Say that again! There's really a Black Forest for sale at your stable? Hey, tell me more about her! What's the name of the ranch again and the name of Sheila's owner?" Marisa was excited. Beth's news sounded very promising.

"There's not much more to tell. It would be best if you call Carlotta Mancini at Mercy Ranch and then come by to see the horse and try her out. I have no idea what she costs. You'd have to discuss that with Carlotta."

"Sure, of course. Hey, I have to talk to my parents first. I'll call you tonight on your home phone. Then you can give me the address and phone number, okay?"

"Sure. I'll talk to you later. Bye!"

"Hey, wait ... Beth? You should ... oh, darn it!"

Beth had already hung up before Marisa could pass along her aunt's message, but, she didn't let that bother her for long. Instead she ran to her parents as fast as possible and overwhelmed them with the news.

"Aunt Nancy says hi, and Beth does too. I found out I could have a mare right now that's at Mercy Ranch where Rondo boards. A Black Forest Shire mare, and she's really sweet, Beth said. But I have no idea how much she costs. Could we go there and look at her? Please!" She was bursting with excitement.

Patrick laughed loudly.

"Tell us the whole story again, this time slowly. Up to now, all I understood was something about a mercy ranch."

"Okay!" Marisa took a breath and tried to get her thoughts in order. When she calmed down she was able to repeat almost word for word what her cousin had said.

"That sounds very promising," responded Mona. "First thing is to get the address and phone number, and then we'll see how far away it is. We can call there and get all the information."

"So at least you're not saying no right away?"

"NO!" her parents shouted back, and Marisa looked puzzled.

"No?"

"Yes, we're not saying no right away!"

"Got it!" Marisa grinned. "Terrific! Thanks a lot!" Then she took off again. She had to sit down in her room with her encyclopedia of horses and read about Black Forest Shire horses. And then she was going to think over whether she could imagine having an animal like that.

"What a question," she thought. "Of course I could!"

* * *

Carlotta had just said good-bye to Dr. Hofer and was now able to breathe a sigh of relief.

The vet had examined Jam again and assured her that

the animal was improving and would soon be back on his feet. That had been Carlotta's main concern and now she had one less worry.

Grateful, she watched the vet's car disappear into the distance, and then she noticed Beth running back from the paddock.

"How's Jam?" she asked, out of breath when she reached Carlotta.

"Everything's okay. Beth, I want to thank you so much for that wonderful present. You had already left when I saw it. It's gorgeous, but you shouldn't have," said Carlotta, but Beth just smiled.

"The main thing is that you like it. I'm so glad. It's just my way of saying thank you. Without you, we, that is Logan and I, would have been out of luck with our horses."

"Well, that was nothing. But, another thing ... were you able to have a talk with Cheryl this morning? You know ..."

Beth shook her head.

"Sorry, I couldn't. She was already gone when I came out. I thought I'd call her tonight."

"That's a good idea, Beth. Do that. I hope she'll be okay soon. The next time she's here, I'm going to try to explain everything to her. Unfortunately, things went badly this morning." Carlotta had a distant look in her eye for a moment, but then she snapped back and was her old self again.

Beth looked at her and asked herself if she should tell her about Marisa but then she decided to talk about Sheila first.

"So you really want to sell Sheila?"

Carlotta nodded.

"Yes, but only if I find someone who will take very good care of her. I owe her that at least, to find her a good home."

"And how much do you want for her? I mean, how much will Sheila cost?"

Carlotta shrugged her shoulders.

"Actually, I haven't even thought about that yet. I think I'm going to make a decision based on finding a good home for her more than getting a lot of money. It's more important to me that she is well taken care of than that I have a few more dollars in my pocket, although I could use some for the ranch, of course," she added honestly.

"I understand." Beth pressed her lips together. Finally she said, "Well, I think I know someone."

Carlotta jumped. She hadn't imagined that things would go this quickly.

"What? Who?"

"My cousin Marisa, who turned fifteen yesterday. Her parents are buying her a horse for her birthday and she's looking for one that would suit her. I told her about Sheila. I hope that's all right, because I heard what you said this morning, and, well, Marisa was really excited. She wants your address and phone number and everything but I haven't given them to her yet. She has to talk with her parents first, and if they approve then she might come here and have a look at Sheila. Would that be all right with you?" There, now she had said it.

"What kind of a person is your cousin?" asked Carlotta.

"Marisa's really nice, and she's always loved horses," said Beth excitedly, just getting started, but Carlotta stopped her and gestured with her head.

"Let's go inside, and then you can tell me more about

her. I want to have a picture of the girl in my mind so I can decide whether she would be a good fit for Sheila."

As they walked across the yard together, Beth realized that she would love it if Marisa bought Sheila.

* * *

"Oh, no, you're not serious, are you? This is a really bad day!" Kevin couldn't stop groaning.

"Hey, could you stop complaining?" asked Ricki. "Once more: The chairs are set far apart. The bucket of water is placed on the last chair and the apple is placed in the bucket. The start is at the first chair. You gallop to the second chair, ride around it, and dismount as quickly as possible. Then you take a deep breath, and put your face down into the water and try to get the apple with your mouth. Then you mount and race back to the start. Then it goes on like a relay race. As soon as the first rider is back, the second one starts off with a new apple. She has to ride around the chair with the apple as fast as possible, put the apple in the bucket, and then ride back, and then the next rider continues the game. There are usually two teams, and the fastest team wins."

"Great game!" Lillian was enthusiastic.

"And if you want to make it a little more difficult, you can do it without a saddle," explained Ricki, "and some people have a lot of trouble trying to get back on the horse with an apple in their mouth, to ride back to the start."

"Well, that wouldn't be a good game for Rashid and me," Cathy shook her head. "First of all, Rashid isn't exactly a small horse, and second, in case you haven't noticed, I'm toting around a few extra pounds that'll slow me down," she smiled, hands on her hips and doing a model turn to show her pleasingly plump shape.

"Well, honestly, I'd rather try this game tomorrow. What other games do you have?" asked Kevin, and he continued to stare at the water bucket.

"Hmmm, well, there's riding with an egg on a spoon. It's like a race carrying an egg, like we did at all those birthday parties when we were little. Just this time on a horse, with a tablespoon and a Ping-Pong ball, which can be pricked and then filled with water, so that it's a little heavier and not so easily knocked off the spoon with a little wind."

"All right! At least you don't get wet doing that! Give me one of those." Kevin reached out his hand.

"Wait a minute, I have to prepare the ball first!" Ricki pulled out a pocketknife and bored a little hole in the Ping-Pong ball. Then she held it in the bucket of water until there were no more bubbles on the surface.

"Finished! Now try your luck. You have to ride to the chair and back, and if you want to be especially good, try it in slalom through the poles."

"Ha, ha! How am I going to do that when I couldn't even do it without this fake egg?" Kevin let her put the ball on his spoon and then Sharazan started off slowly.

"A little faster, please!" called out Lillian, happily. "If you go that slow, an ant could catch you."

"Go, Kevin – go, Kevin – go – go – go!" Ricki and Cathy began to cheer on the boy in unison, but instead of motivating him, the noise seemed to make him nervous.

"You guys are driving me crazy!" he yelled, and there would have been scrambled egg if he had had a real egg on his spoon.

The girls all laughed.

"Come on, try again! We can't believe you can't even make it for that short distance!" Kevin began to feel competitive.

"Hey, come back!" Lillian waved at him. "I'll ride with you. Let's see who wins!"

"Okay! Just you wait! You don't stand a chance!" Kevin risked saying as Ricki filled up a second ball.

"And when you get back, then it's our turn, okay, Cathy?"

"Sure!" she yelled in a good mood.

"Okay, Lillian, I'm done." Ricki gave her a spoon with a ball, too, and then Sharazan and Holli stood next to one another and Ricki shouted, "On your marks, get set, gooooo!"

"Oh, it really is hard." Lillian almost bit her lip, she was concentrating so hard, but she kept Holli in a calm walk, while Kevin wanted to show off what he could do, and he urged Sharazan into a trot.

He was just able to keep his ball on the spoon as they trotted along, until Sharazan shook his head to get rid of some flies, and then it was all over.

"How mean!" he laughed, and then he tried, unfairly, to get Lillian to laugh as well, but the girl managed to get across the finish line with her ball still on the spoon.

"And the winner isssss Lilliannnnn!" screamed Ricki. Then she mounted Diablo's saddle for her turn. "Okay, give me those eggs! Cathy, are you ready? Can we start?"

Rashid's rider nodded and Kevin counted slowly, "One – two – three– start!"

"Oh man, oh man, oh man, this isn't going to work!" whined Cathy, who was already having trouble holding the spoon still for the first few yards. Ricki was doing pretty well. She had an advantage in that Diablo's gait was more like a rocking chair than a horse. He was easy to sit on and Ricki was hardly wobbling at all.

"Hey, I don't know what your problem is! This is really eassssss – Oh, it's not that easy after all!" she laughed, as the ball bounced between her horse's feet.

"Hey, what are you guys doing? I can hear you from a mile away!" It was Josh, who sat confidently in his Western saddle on his pinto mare, Cherish. He had been watching from the entrance to the paddock for quite a while, unnoticed.

"Josh!" Lillian's eyes began to shine, and she quickly led Holli in a trot over to her boyfriend. "How long have you been here? We didn't see you arrive!" she said, surprised. She was so glad to see him.

"You were concentrating so hard on what you were doing," he laughed. "Are you guys practicing for the games tournament?"

"You got the invitation, too?"

"Of course! So, how's it going?" he asked, looking at Ricki and Cathy with interest, as they tried again.

"Hmmm, well, to be honest, I think we don't really have much talent for this sort of thing," Lillian admitted readily.

"It's just a matter of practicing. For example, riding in slalom. It's not as difficult as it looks." Slowly, Josh rode Cherish toward the plastic poles, and easily rode zigzag around all of them with only one hand on the reins. Then he turned and trotted back the same way.

"What about at a gallop?" Kevin wanted to know.

"No different," answered Josh.

"Then do it!"

"Oh, I don't want to depress you."

"Nothing will shock me today. Come on, I want to see a gallop!"

Josh shrugged his shoulders, and then he let Cherish gallop and surge forward through the poles in an unbeatable best time.

"Wow! That was really great." Ricki nodded at him admiringly.

"Hah, that's just due to the horse," remarked Kevin, and Josh dismounted immediately.

"Come on. Let's exchange horses," he winked at him. "You ride Cherish, and I'll try it on Sharazan."

"Done!" Kevin jumped out of the saddle and walked over to Cherish. "My lady, don't disappoint me!"

"Kevin is weird today, don't you think?" Cathy commented to Ricki.

"If it doesn't get any worse, I can live with it," she replied, and then she watched both rides, enthralled. "This is going to be interesting. I'm really curious to see if this works."

"Okay, who wants to go first?" Josh called out, and Kevin pointed down at Cherish. "Ladies first!" he shouted and steered the little pinto mare through the poles in a slow gait.

"That wasn't bad, was it?" he asked, looking for praise.

"At a walk!" grinned Josh. "Cherish could do that blindfolded!" Then he started Sharazan. He rode using both hands, but he left the reins relatively long and used his body weight as aids. It was so effective that the roan reacted wonderfully and managed it easily.

Kevin was bewildered.

"He's betraying me," he complained. "Did you see that? Sharazan, you beast! How come you won't do that with me?"

"And now trot," Josh ordered, and again, Kevin rode first. He worked the reins too energetically and almost confused Cherish, but since she was a well-trained Western horse she sensed what he wanted her to do, and so Kevin managed to do it again.

"I'm going to try it at a gallop," the boy called out, now overconfident, but apparently Cherish had had enough and simply refused to budge. No matter what Kevin did, she just stood still, like a stubborn mule, and wouldn't move.

Josh laughed until the tears came, and then he started off at a trot with Sharazan. With a little effort, he managed to do it.

"He isn't used to doing this, and it would be ridiculous to try to force him through at a gallop," the young man said, afterward. "I could make him mad and then it would be hard to get him to do a slalom race afterward. It's better to stop now. He did really well!" He praised Sharazan and patted his neck and then he jumped down from the saddle.

"I can see that if you come we won't stand a chance, just as I thought." Ricki looked at her watch. "My goodness, it's been more than two hours! I think we'd better stop for today. We can continue tomorrow. It's going to take a while to get everything back to the stable. Is that okay with all of you?"

Cathy came over on Rashid.

"You wanted me to explain math to you," she reminded her friend, who had conveniently let her least favorite subject slip her mind.

"Oh, no! I completely forgot. Darn it!" she said with a touch of sarcasm, slapping her hand against her forehead.

"Yeah, life isn't just about riding," said Josh with sympathy.

"It's easy for you to say. After all, you're already finished with boring high school."

"And I'm glad!" He smiled at Lillian. "I'm going to take off, if Kevin manages to bring back my horse. Hey Kevin, are you planning to spend the night out there?"

Ricki's boyfriend scowled desperately.

"It's as though I'm sitting on a big rock! She won't budge!" he complained.

"Cherish!" called Josh, laughing, and whistled softly.

Immediately, the mare's head shot up.

"Come!"

Cherish came quickly, without even a thought for her rider.

"This beast is spooky!" Kevin was in awe.

"She's just well trained," Lillian's boyfriend corrected him, before disappearing from their sight with Cherish at a light gallop.

***

It was almost 4 o'clock when Logan arrived at Mercy Ranch. As the day wore on, Beth had decided that he wasn't able to make it after all, so when he did show up she was even happier to see him.

"How did it go? Did you finish?" she asked, full of curiosity.

Logan nodded.

"Yeah. Everything's all set. All ready for tomorrow. There's even feed in the racks," he added, winking. "Our two horses will feel right at home when they enter their new stalls."

Beth was delighted.

She took Logan's hand and both of them ran into the stable.

"Jam's much better. He didn't look that good this morning, but now he's even chewing a little hay."

"That's great. The poor guy. What else is new? Anything I should know?"

Beth nodded. "Sheila's going to be sold and Cheryl is totally upset. She rode home right after she heard. But you know what might be good? My cousin's parents are buying her a horse for her birthday, and I thought maybe I could interest her in Sheila. We'll see if it works out."

"Your cousin?"

"Yeah. My cousin Marisa. I think she and Sheila would get along well."

"Better than Cheryl and Sheila?" Logan asked after a little hesitation.

Beth shrugged her shoulders.

"That's a question that really makes me feel guilty. Can't you ask me something else?"

Logan smiled.

"Of course! Did you miss me?"

Beth beamed at him.

"*That* was a good question!" As a reply, she gave him a soft kiss on the cheek. "By the way, I already groomed Star for you. However, it's hard to tell now, because when I took him to the paddock to be with Rondo, he rolled in the dirt right away, and so it was all for nothing."

"Ah, yes, that's the fate of snow-white horses!" sighed Logan. "Still, thanks a lot for your efforts. Actually, I wanted to go riding a little, but, to be honest, I don't really feel like brushing out the grass stains first. Did you go out riding today?"

Beth nodded. "Yeah, but not for long."

"What do you think about us starting the stall work now? It looks as though we're going to be alone here today."

"Oh, I think Kieran will show up. If not, it would be the first time he didn't come to the ranch. Bev might come, too, although ever since Carlotta threw her friend Lena off the property, she doesn't show up very often."

"That's true. But you know, when we're gone, it's going to be really empty here. I hope that Cheryl is able to get over losing Sheila, because if she doesn't come back either, there isn't going to be enough help for the stable work. Carlotta might have to hire someone; it would be too much for her."

"Okay, but if we keep standing here much longer and talking, we're not going to be much help either. Let's get started!"

***

Cheryl lay on her bed and cried her eyes out. After she left the ranch in such a hurry, she rode all over the area on her bike, following almost every path she had ridden with Sheila, her heart heavy with all her problems involving Carlotta, and the world.

Why? She kept asking herself. *Why does it have to be Sheila that's going to be sold?*

Once back home, she went to her room and spread out all the photos that she had taken of her darling horse. There was Sheila in the paddock, in the stall, with her at the riding ring ... A photo that Cheryl found especially beautiful was one that Cathy had taken about a month ago, after they had returned from riding together. It was a close-up of Cheryl as she hugged Sheila's neck, her face beaming.

Under other circumstances, she could have gone on looking at the photo for hours, because the mare was so beautiful and her eyes looked so happy and contented. Today, however, she couldn't bear to glance at it for more than a second. If she looked any more it would break her heart, and so she put it away in the lowest drawer of her bureau.

She would never be as happy as she looked in that photo.

The door to her room opened softly and her mother came in.

"Are you going to tell me yet what's wrong?" asked her mother gently, sitting down next to her daughter on the bed.

Cheryl shook her head without looking up.

Her mother looked around the room. The photos of Sheila were lying everywhere, and slowly she began to realize what was making her daughter so unhappy.

"What's happening with Sheila?" she asked softly, and put her hand on Cheryl's back, and instinctively began stroking it. When her daughter had been small, this touch had been enough to comfort her.

Cheryl sobbed. Suddenly she sat up and threw herself into her mother's arms.

"Is it so awful?" asked Mrs. Vincent, whispering.

"Oh, Mom, Sheila's going to be sold! That ... that is so, so terrible! I can't stand it! It's so mean!" Cheryl stammered, tears streaming down her cheeks.

"But why?"

The girl shrugged her shoulders weakly.

"I have no idea."

Mrs. Vincent sighed.

"Mom, can't we buy Sheila?" asked Cheryl, a small

glimmer of hope in her red eyes. "I could get a job after school. I could deliver the newspaper or shelve at the supermarket, or ... or anything to pay for her board."

"Cheryl, the money that you made would never be enough to pay for a horse's upkeep. Think over what you yourself told me just a while ago: rent for the stall is expensive, then there's the feed, shots, vet, blacksmith, and more. It all costs an enormous amount of money. And finally, we would have to have the money to buy the horse." She paused before continuing. "And you know that we just don't have it."

A new stream of tears ran down Cheryl's face.

"I'm so sorry, honey," said Andrea Vincent, "but, as much as I would like to make this wish come true for you, it's impossible."

Cheryl fell back onto the bed.

"It would be my biggest wish," she whispered hoarsely and stared at the ceiling through her tears. "The biggest and the only wish of my life."

"I know."

"If Sheila isn't there any more, then ..."

"Cheryl, I know that this is going to sound silly to you, and that you probably don't want to hear this right now, but even if Sheila is sold, life goes on, and some day you will fall in love with another horse, and love it just as much."

"No, Mom! Oh, you just don't understand!" Cheryl turned her face to the wall. All she wanted now was to be alone with her sadness. There was no one who could comfort her over the loss of Sheila, and she would never go near a stable again.

Chapter 5

"Well, why didn't you tell me sooner that you're in such a financially tight situation?" asked Eleanor Highland, the owner of Highland Farms Estate and a dear friend of Carlotta's, as they spoke on the phone.

"What would that have changed? You know how I am. I always manage somehow."

"Oh, yes! You always manage, even if it means that you have to do without! That's how it's been ever since I've known you. However, what help can you be if you ruin your health? Please, hire a full-time stable hand now."

"I can't afford one right now. Well, now that I'm not going to be able to build the riding hall, I'll have a little extra, but ..."

Mrs. Charles Osgood Highland III interrupted rigorously.

"Now you listen to me, Carlotta Mancini! I think your involvement with Mercy Ranch is wonderful, but you shouldn't always try to do everything yourself. Look, you have a few empty stalls in your stable, and if I know you it's only a matter of time before you find more poor, neglected creatures to fill them. How are you going to manage? I mean, I'm sure your young stable assistants are fabulous, but at some point they're going to get older and have other interests, and then where will you be? They don't give you any guarantees. I see this every day with Gwendolyn. My darling granddaughter has her head filled with dreams. Today she wants to do this, tomorrow something else. No, Carlotta, you're going to have to hire a full-time groom."

Carlotta sighed. She had thought this matter over a thousand times, but had always pushed it aside. She knew, however, that her friend was right.

Sure, if she were a few years younger, everything would be different, but she just couldn't get used to the idea that she would need to have a fixed sum of money every month to pay a ranch hand.

Mrs. Highland could almost hear her friend thinking. She knew Carlotta was a proud woman and wouldn't consider taking financial help from a friend, even as a loan.

"I have an idea," Mrs. Highland offered after a few moments. "How about this? You look for someone to help out, and when you find that person, I'll send you a donation for the ranch to cover his wages for one year. Wouldn't that be a good solution?"

Carlotta objected immediately. "You want to pay for my employee? I won't allow it!"

Mrs. Highland chuckled. "Carlotta, we've been friends for longer than we both care to admit. You know I never worry about whether others are willing to allow something or not. Anyway, as I already said, it would be a donation –

well, let's say, with the stipulation that you really do hire someone. Oh, yes, and before you get upset again, please remember that I can deduct donations from my taxes if you give me a receipt for the money."

"You're impossible!" Carlotta finally gave up.

"I know, but you're not much better!"

* * *

While Ricki poured over her math workbook with Cathy and realized that she'd never be able to understand the subject, Beth called her cousin to give her Carlotta's address.

"Hey, do you have e-mail? Then I can send you a photo of Sheila if you want," Beth offered.

"That would be fantastic!"

So now Marisa sat in front of her computer, waiting for an e-mail to arrive. It seemed like an eternity before she heard the ding that notified her of an incoming e-mail.

I can't wait to see her, Marisa thought, and downloaded the data. *Darn this stupid modem. This is taking forever! Beth should have made the photo a little smaller.*

The minutes ticked by, and Marisa tried to imagine what Sheila looked like. True, her cousin had described her pretty well, but when she finally opened the e-mail she discovered that Arabian horses don't all look the same and neither do Black Forest horses.

She stared at an amazing white Arabian and a beautiful Black Forest Shire mare, a little smaller than was typical for the breed. At first she didn't even notice the two people who were also in the photo, standing next to the horses and smiling at the camera.

That's my boyfriend, Logan, with his Star, and next to him is Cheryl and Sheila. Cheryl is a friend of mine and has taken care of Sheila for a long time. She rides her almost every day, Beth had added to the e-mail.

She looks nice, thought Marisa, looking briefly at the girl. Then she enlarged the part of the photo with Sheila and printed it right away.

Finally, she had a photo of the mare that was for sale, and Marisa had to admit that she had fallen in love with the horse at first sight. She dialed Beth's cell phone number right away.

"Hey, she looks really sweet. And is she really as easy to ride and manage as you said? It's too bad you don't know what she costs. I'm pretty sure Dad isn't going to want to make the long drive to Mercy Ranch if he doesn't know the price in advance."

"You'll have to call Carlotta to make an appointment anyway. Then he can ask her," Beth replied, and Marisa felt silly.

"You're right! I think I'm starting to go crazy with all this concentration on horses." The girl laughed. "You know, I'm already starting to imagine what it would be like to ride through the countryside here on Sheila."

Beth smiled knowingly.

"I can imagine. That's the way I was with Rondo. From the first moment I saw him, until he was finally in my stable, I rode him in my mind hundreds of times, groomed him, and imagined all kinds of adventures we would have. I think that's normal," she added, sharing her cousin's excitement.

"Thanks so much, Beth. I'll call as soon as I know anything for sure. Sorry to be hanging up so soon, but I can't wait to show Sheila's photo to Mom and Dad. I can't wait to hear what they think."

"That's okay!" responded Beth understandingly. "I've got to go, too. I want to call Cheryl."

"Oh, dear. She's got to be really sad that her foster horse is being sold, isn't she?"

"She's not just sad, she's completely destroyed. That's why I want to call her and try to cheer her up a little, if that's possible."

Marisa was silent a few seconds. "You know what? Now I feel very guilty," she said softly.

But Beth tried to get her cousin to see the reality of the situation.

"You don't have to. Look, Sheila's going to be sold, no matter what, either to you or to someone else, but it would be better if she went to you, because then Cheryl can be sure that she's going to be well taken care of, and that's the main thing!"

"Yeah, that's true, too. And Beth, you know she would be better off with me than with anyone else."

"I know. Anyway, good luck. And tell Aunt Mona and Uncle Patrick I said hello," Beth said before hanging up. She really hoped for Marisa's sake, as well as for Sheila, that things would work out.

***

When the kids met at the picnic tables near the bike stands at school the next day for lunch, Ricki and her friends found out from Beth that Sheila was going to be sold.

"Are you sure? How long have you known?" asked Lillian, very surprised by the news.

"Yes, I'm sure. Carlotta told us yesterday. Right afterward, Cheryl ran off and we haven't seen her since."

"I can imagine it's pretty rough on her," said Cathy nodding sympathetically, before looking around.

"Have you guys seen her today?"

"No."

"I called her last night, but her mom said she didn't want to talk to me. She shut herself in her room and wouldn't talk to anyone," Beth told them.

"Then she's really upset! I can totally understand."

"Maybe we should go see her today after school," suggested Kevin, after thinking about it briefly.

"Do you think that would be a good idea?" asked Ricki in response. "If it were me, I would want to be alone with my feelings and to deal with the fact that my horse was being sold."

Beth shrugged. "Well, I don't know. That's how I felt when my father sold Rondo, but then I was really glad that I met you guys and could talk to you about it."

"Okay, then let's meet in town later this afternoon. We can go see Cheryl and then we can ride our bikes to Mercy Ranch. It'll probably be too late to go riding, but I doubt our horses will be unhappy spending another day on the paddock," responded Ricki.

"And I'll get out of having to play that bucket of water with the apple game!" Kevin winked at his girlfriend.

"Oh, now I know why you're feeling so sorry for Cheryl. You just want to get out of playing that game!"

"No way. But it's a nice side benefit."

"You know, it's just a delay, not a cancellation. If not today, then tomorrow, or the day after, or –"

"Or I'll just decide not to participate in the tournament! It looks to me as though the audience will have more fun and more to laugh about than the riders."

"I don't think so. I think the games are really fun, whether you're taking part or just watching. Anyway, I'm looking forward to it, and I hope there are enough people registered so the tournament can happen." said a determined Lillian, and Ricki and Cathy both gave a thumbs-up in agreement.

Beth looked from one to the other, bewildered.

"I don't understand a word you just said! What are you guys talking about?"

"The Fun and Games Festival that's being put on by the riding club. We'll tell you all about it later, okay?"

"Okay!"

Classes were about to resume after the lunch break, so the friends cleared their sandwich wrappers and soda cans off the table and headed back inside, but the thought of Cheryl's despair touched them all.

* * *

"Maybe we can talk Cheryl into practicing for the games tournament, too! Not with Sheila, but with another horse. That would be a good distraction for her, and she could get used to another horse," Lillian suggested on the way home later.

"Do you really think she'd feel like doing that right now?" Ricki wondered aloud. "And apart from that, I can't imagine she'd be willing to ride another horse, at least as long as Sheila's still at Carlotta's ranch. She would never do that to Sheila," Ricki added.

"Maybe, but we can try, anyway."

"Which horse should she train on? After all, Sheila is the only horse at Mercy Ranch who doesn't have a handicap. Most of the horses are really old or they have problems with their joints, and the rapid turns would be awful for them," chimed in Cathy.

"That's true, but if necessary, she can practice on Holli. I think the most important thing is for her to be distracted a little."

Ricki laughed.

"Kevin doesn't want to take part in the tournament anyway. Maybe she could ride Sharazan. I'll have to ask him later, when we're in town."

"That's a thought," Lillian giggled. "Your Romeo just can't do it!"

Just as Ricki was about to reply, her cell phone rang. She quickly stopped her bike, so as not to miss the call.

"Hi, Ricki, it's Beth. I completely forgot that we're going to bring the horses to the new stable today so we can't go to Cheryl's with you guys. Sorry I didn't think of it sooner."

Ricki nodded.

"I wondered about that. Okay then, have fun. See you later."

"Absolutely! Maybe we'll go over to Mercy Ranch early tonight. We still have to get all the grooming equipment. Say hi to Cheryl for us, okay?"

"Sure! See you later."

Ricki hung up and told Lillian about Beth's call before they separated to go to their own homes.

"What would happen," Lillian wondered, "if Logan and Beth broke up and she had Rondo at his stable? Wouldn't that be awkward?"

"That would definitely be awkward, but it's as if the two of them are made for each other. They really suit each other," said Ricki, and Lillian had to smile.

"You've completely changed your mind about Logan, haven't you?"

"Oh, definitely, yes! Don't remind me about how I acted when he first moved here. I've apologized a thousand times for that," groaned Ricki. Then she pedaled fiercely to get up the little hill to her parent's farm.

* * *

Cheryl had become so obsessed about losing Sheila that she couldn't go to school Monday morning. She had lain awake the whole night and cried, and when the alarm clock rang at six a.m. she felt sick to her stomach.

"I understand that this is upsetting you," Andrea Vincent tried to soothe her daughter when she went into Cheryl's room to see why she hadn't gotten up yet, "but you can't let yourself go like this. I know Shelia is important to you, but your education is more important. You know that. You can't stay home just because a horse is being sold!"

"A horse! Just a horse! It's Sheila, Mom! Sheila!"

"Even if it is Sheila, you're going to school!" Mrs. Vincent was emphatic.

"But I feel sick to my stomach! You just don't understand. I can't go today!"

"Yes, you can. You're just feeling sick because you won't stop thinking about that horse. If you go to school, you'll be distracted. Just look at it like that for now. Now, get up, please, and get dressed! I don't want you to be late." Andrea pulled back the blanket roughly and left the room.

Cheryl could have screamed, but it wouldn't have changed anything – neither her mother's mind nor the fact that Shelia would soon be gone. She forced herself to get up and get dressed.

Without saying good-bye to her mother, she walked past the kitchen and left the house.

When Andrea Vincent heard the door shut, she looked out the window and sighed. She understood Cheryl better than her daughter knew, and so she forgave her for leaving without a word.

By this afternoon, she'll have dealt with it, she thought, as Cheryl rode her bike down the driveway and onto the road in the direction of school.

Thousands of thoughts raced through the girl's head, and when Cheryl saw the school in front of her, she hesitated, and then turned off onto a side street. No! She wouldn't be able to concentrate anyway, and having to see the pity on the faces of her friends made the tears well up yet again.

"Carlotta just can't sell Sheila!" she murmured to herself, choking, and she started riding around hoping for a miracle, for some fairy godmother to grant her wish. She thought of all the fairy tales she knew, and when she came to *Aladdin and the Magic Lamp,* she stopped and looked heavenward.

"Dear God," she prayed softly. "I know that there are no fairies and no genies, but if there is anything you can do so that Sheila stays at the ranch, then please do it! Please!"

* * *

Marisa couldn't pay attention at school that morning. Her thoughts kept returning to Sheila and to her father, who had promised her that he would call Carlotta that morning.

"That's really a nice little horse," her father had said after he saw the photo of Sheila. "But not cheap, I'll bet," he added, scaring Marisa.

"How much can my horse cost?" Marisa had asked cautiously.

"You know it's not right to talk about the price of a present," was her father's reply. Now she could only hope the price wouldn't be too high, and that owning Sheila wouldn't become a shattered dream.

When Marisa returned home at the end of the school day, she ran right into her father's office.

"So? Did you talk to her? What did she say?" she burst out immediately.

"Hello, daughter! How about taking a breath and giving your dad a hug?" Patrick laughed, but just by reading his facial expression, Marisa could tell that her chances of getting Sheila were good.

Overwhelmed with happiness, she gave him a huge bear hug.

"Hey, hey, hey – I didn't say anything yet!" Patrick freed himself from her embrace, panting.

"Your eyes speak volumes! Come on, tell me, when are we going to that ranch?"

"Ask my eyes," teased Patrick, but then he decided not to keep Marisa in suspense. "How about tomorrow afternoon, after school?"

"Yes! Yes! Yes!" Marisa almost turned cartwheels for joy. "Oh, Dad, I'm so excited! Say, what's she like, this Mrs. Mancini? Is she nice? And, I know you can't talk about money and presents, but is the price okay? Oh, wow, I think I'm going to go crazy! Have I told you that I have the best parents in the world? And that I'm going to look at a horse tomorrow?"

"Oh, really?" Patrick was just able to block a wet kiss, and then, without waiting another second, Marisa took off to look for her mother.

Lovingly, Marisa's father watched her go, and then later he said to his wife, "I don't think I've ever seen that kid so happy!"

* * *

Carlotta was pleasantly surprised when Patrick Swinton called her that morning. He had made an extremely good impression, and if his daughter was half as nice, then Sheila really did have a chance of getting a good home. However, Carlotta knew from long experience that being nice on the telephone wasn't the same thing as being a horse lover, and therefore she was going to wait until she met the Swinton family before making any further judgments. Her first impression certainly matched everything that Beth had told her about Marisa and her parents.

"Well, we'll see tomorrow," murmured Carlotta, a little sadly to herself. Leaving her house with a long list of things she needed to accomplish buzzing in her brain, she decided first to go and have a look at the paddock, where Sheila and her fellow horses were grazing peacefully.

Lost in thought, she stopped short when she saw Cheryl standing in front of the paddock. The girl was leaning her arms on the fence with her head buried in her arms. Sheila stood near her and affectionately blew into her hair with her nostrils.

Slowly Carlotta limped across the yard to her on her crutches, which she'd needed since a riding accident many years ago. She stopped behind the girl without Cheryl noticing her.

"What are you doing here at the ranch at this time of day? Shouldn't you be in school?" she asked, her voice gentle, already knowing what had driven the girl to come here.

Startled, Cheryl turned around, and Sheila jumped aside and galloped away.

"I ... I ..." she stammered, and then she shrugged her shoulders helplessly. "I couldn't go to school! I couldn't stop thinking about Sheila, and that she's going to be sold."

"Hmmm."

Cheryl's eyes followed her foster horse.

"I never wanted to come here again. I didn't want to ever go into a horse stable again, and look how long I managed to stay away. The thought that Sheila will be gone soon and that I will never see her again is driving me crazy. Oh, Carlotta, please, please, don't sell her! I'll die if she isn't here anymore!" Cheryl stared at Carlotta with a look that went right through her.

"I know, it's not easy, child ... Come with me and let's talk about it, okay?"

Cheryl closed her fingers around the fence pole. Carlotta had said, "Let's talk about it!" Did that mean that there was a teeny tiny chance that she could keep Sheila?

With hope in her heart, Cheryl followed the ranch owner into her house. It was a very difficult walk, because she didn't know what to expect.

* * *

Andrea Vincent was terribly upset when she found her daughter's riding companions at the door, asking how she was and wanting to see her.

"She wasn't at school? Oh, no. She left for school this morning but hasn't come home yet. She said she felt sick to her stomach this morning. Oh, I wish I'd let her stay home after all. I shouldn't have insisted that she go to school. Maybe she fell somewhere and –" The woman covered her eyes with her hands as the friends looked on in shock.

"But if that were the case, you would have been notified already," Lillian, who had regained her composure first, tried to be logical, and to calm Cheryl's mother's fears. Unfortunately, she achieved just the opposite.

"At least I'd know where she is! This way – Heavens, what am I going to do? And all because of that horse!" Andrea Vincent's nerves were frayed. However, the word "horse" gave Cheryl's friends some clues to her whereabouts.

"Maybe she just rode around, waited for school to be over, and then went to Beth's. She's her best friend."

"Best friend! That might be, but yesterday, when Beth called, Cheryl didn't even want to talk to her. She didn't want to talk to anyone. She locked herself in her room."

"Oh, no," said Ricki and bit her lip. "Maybe she rode out to Mercy Ranch," was her new suggestion.

Andrea Vincent stared at Ricki intensely, and then she became animated.

"I should have thought of that myself! That would be the most logical place. Does anyone know the phone number there? I'm going to call right away."

Kevin nodded and reached for his cell phone, and he followed Cheryl's mother to the kitchen phone to give her the number. The others waited in the family room. When he came back he joined his friends and they all waited anxiously to see what the conversation with Carlotta would reveal.

A few minutes later, Mrs. Vincent appeared.

"You were right!" she said tensely. "Cheryl was at the ranch, but at ten o'clock this morning. Apparently Mrs. Mancini had a long conversation with her and tried to explain why she was selling the horse, and then Cheryl, completely upset, rode away on her bike and, of course, she didn't say where she was going."

"But at least we know now that she didn't collapse somewhere," Cathy dared to say, and earned a helpless look from Cheryl's mother.

"That doesn't help me at all, right now. Who knows where that girl is!"

Kevin was still holding his cell phone when Ricki pointed at it.

"Call Beth. Maybe Cheryl went there after all," she said to her boyfriend. While it was still ringing, everyone stared at the boy, who was listening intensely.

"Hey, Beth, one question. Was or is Cheryl at your house? No? Darn it! She's disappeared and no one knows where she is ... What? ... Yeah ... I'll talk to you later. Bye!" Slowly Kevin lowered the phone.

"And now?" Cathy looked as terrified as Cheryl's mother.

"I'd really like to call the police," Mrs. Vincent said.

"Mrs. Vincent, I think she's just holed up somewhere to be alone, so that she can deal with the Sheila situation," said Lillian, trying to calm her.

"Let's hope so, but I won't have a moment's peace until I know where she is, or until she's back home."

"Of, course!"

Ricki looked around the room.

"What do you think of us looking for her? After all, we know all the places where we like to hide sometimes when we're feeling down."

Kevin nodded.

"That's a good idea, but we're not going to be able to get around to all the places on our bikes."

"That's true. Let's ride back home and saddle the horses."

"Okay!"

Andrea Vincent nodded her approval of the idea.

"Thank you!" she said, softly. "And if you find her, please let me know immediately."

"Yes, of course!" Kevin smiled encouragingly at the woman. "She's probably sitting somewhere and doesn't even realize that you're here scared to death."

"I'm sure we'll find her," Ricki said with confidence, trying to make Cheryl's mother feel better.

Lillian searched in her jeans pocket and finally found a little pencil with which she wrote something on a piece of paper.

"Here," she said, and held it out to Mrs. Vincent. "That's my cell phone number. If Cheryl comes home in the meantime, then you can call us."

"I will. Good luck! And once again, thanks, all of you. You're being so kind!"

"No problem, Mrs. Vincent. Of course we'll look for her – Cheryl's our friend."

Without further delay, the four friends got back on their bikes and rode to the stable as quickly as they could. They would brush their horses before they rode off, but not for as long as usual. Lillian knew that today it would look like she was riding a grass-green horse instead of a white one, but that wasn't important now. The only thing that mattered was finding Cheryl.

Chapter 6

Beth and Logan were at Mercy Ranch saddling their horses in their stalls. The thought that after this ride they would no longer be returning here gave them a strange feeling in the pits of their stomachs. Nevertheless, they were excited to be moving to the new stable.

Unfortunately, Beth's happiness was further dampened by Cheryl's disappearance. She kept thinking of her friend, and wondering where she could be. She had already tried to reach her on her cell phone several times, but it seemed that Cheryl had turned it off.

"Well, you two, the time has come," said Carlotta, who had come with a fat carrot for each of the horses as a good-bye present.

Logan nodded. "Yes, I guess so. Carlotta, I want to thank you again – for everything."

"Me, too!" Beth joined in. She would have liked to say more, but she had an enormous lump in her throat that made it almost impossible to speak.

She gave the ranch owner a huge hug.

"I'm going to miss you, and the stable, and all of the horses as well!" she finally managed to say, her voice almost breaking.

"I'll miss you, too, but if I know you, you'll be coming by more often than you think." Carlotta gently eased Beth away and smiled at her. "Don't worry, I'm sure we'll see each other again soon."

Logan grinned.

"Of course! Tonight, at least, when we pick up our grooming kits."

Carlotta nodded, and then she voiced her concern about the missing girl.

"You still haven't reached Cheryl?" she asked Beth, who had to say no.

"Please keep your eyes open on the ride. If you happen to see her, please tell her that she has to call her mother or, better yet, go home. Mrs. Vincent is terribly worried."

"We will!" Beth promised, and then she grabbed Rondo's reins and led her horse out of the stall.

"See you, Carlotta!" she said, and Logan waved again, before leading Star behind Rondo.

Outside, in front of the stable, the two teens tightened their girths before swinging up into the saddle and trotting off, away from the ranch.

"Good luck, you two," said Carlotta, softly. "And find that girl for me!" She felt guilty that Cheryl had taken Sheila's sale so badly and run off.

Once again she went over the conversation she had had with her.

Cheryl had pleaded with her several times not to sell

Sheila. She had thought of all kinds of ways to earn money so that she could buy the mare herself, but it was impossible for Carlotta to give in. She couldn't sell a horse to a fourteen-year-old, and even if she could, it would have been impossible for Cheryl to come up with the necessary money, even if Carlotta kept the price to the minimum. And so, as much as she had hated to do it, she had had to crush Cheryl's hopes of having Sheila as her own.

Carlotta took a deep breath, and slowly walked back to the stable, staring pensively at Sheila as she sat down on the little bench in the corridor.

She just sat there for a while, thinking, trying to see whether there was a solution to the problem after all.

Of course, the easiest thing would be to just not sell the animal, but that would go against the ground rules she had set for herself when she had started Mercy Ranch. She had decided then to find good homes for various horses so that she would have room for more neglected creatures that needed her help and care.

"She'll get over it," Carlotta tried to convince herself, but her heart knew differently. Then she thought of the following day, when Beth's relatives were scheduled to come and take a look at Sheila.

Maybe it was a mistake to tell Cheryl about that, she thought. *But, on the other hand, I thought that it would be easier to say good-bye to Sheila, if she knew that she would have a good home.* Yet nothing could be further from the truth. Apparently, her openness had just made everything worse.

Carlotta sighed. She could spin it any way she chose; Cheryl would have to get used to the idea that Sheila was going to a new home.

She got up wearily and pushed the wheelbarrow with the manure in front of Rondo's box.

Although Beth and Logan wanted to come by later to clean out the boxes, Carlotta got started on the work anyway. She had to do something to distract herself, because Cheryl's sadness when she'd left the ranch that morning, and the fact that she had disappeared, were hard for her to bear. She couldn't help feeling responsible.

* * *

Cheryl sat along the bank of Echo Lake, in a secluded spot invisible from the woods, and stared at the surface of the water. After riding around for a long time, she had decided to come here, and had thrown her bike with her school backpack carelessly into the bushes. She had been sitting there, in the shade of a hazelnut tree, for hours. Every once in a while, she stretched her legs a bit and then returned to her motionless state.

In her mind, she replayed almost every minute of the times she had spent with Sheila.

She thought back to how everything had begun and remembered that she had always loved Black Forest Shire horses especially, and had dreamed of owning or at least riding such a horse one day. It had been through the silliness of a former girlfriend that she had come to know Carlotta, and she was asked to exercise Rashid when Cathy had been unable to ride after an accident. Later, when Cathy was able to take over caring for the dun horse again, Cheryl could hardly believe her luck when Carlotta permitted her to care for and ride her dream horse, Sheila, whenever she felt like it.

Sheila had been extremely shy with people, due to

the harsh treatment of her previous owner, and in the beginning Cheryl had to be very careful not to get bitten or kicked. But Carlotta and Cheryl had managed to win the horse's trust fairly quickly, and after that Sheila had developed into an extremely gentle animal. Even a child could ride her now or play in her stall without any fear of getting hurt.

Cheryl blew her nose noisily, and thought about how incredibly happy she had been.

Now, she wondered how many tears a person could possibly shed, as she continued to remember everything that had happened.

So many wonderful rides she had taken on the horse, to the most beautiful spots in the area ... even here, near where she was sitting now. She had been here with Sheila just a few days ago, had embraced her beautiful head and promised her that nothing would ever separate them, and now ... she wouldn't be able to keep her promise.

Carlotta had destroyed her happiness. Even though, deep down, Cheryl knew that it had been very difficult for the Mercy Ranch owner to let the animal go, she also knew that she would never forgive Carlotta if she sold Sheila. In doing so, Carlotta would be taking away the very thing that meant the most to her. She would never get over the loss of Sheila. Never!

* * *

Ricki and her friends had searched for Cheryl in all the likely places, but hadn't found her.

"She has to be somewhere!" said Lillian and halted her white Hanoverian. "She can't have just disappeared into thin air."

"Maybe she's not outdoors. Maybe she's at someone's house crying her eyes out," suggested Kevin.

"At whose house? I would have thought maybe at Beth's, but, first of all, Beth's not home, and secondly, I bet Cheryl's pretty mad at her if Beth brought her cousin into this as a possible buyer for Sheila."

"Does Cheryl know that?"

"I have no idea, but it's possible, isn't it?"

Ricki looked questioningly at Cathy.

"Maybe Carlotta told her. But anyway, if I were Cheryl, I'd go someplace where I could be alone. Then I'd probably start feeling betrayed by everything and everyone, and I'd be glad that no one could see me."

"Oh, she really could be anywhere, and if we keep standing around here much longer and talking about it, we're never going to find her!" responded Kevin.

"If we ever do find her," replied Cathy.

Lillian and Ricki looked at each other.

"I think it would be best if we separated," suggested Lillian. "Cathy and I can ride through the woods and out into the fields to that old shed where we always stop for a rest when we go riding together. Maybe Cheryl shut herself in there. You two can keep looking around here. After all, we haven't searched every single spot yet."

Ricki nodded.

"Yeah! Let's do that. Good luck, everybody!"

"Ditto!"

Lillian and Cathy turned their horses around and onto a path that would eventually take them out of the woods.

Ricki and her boyfriend kept riding straight ahead.

"This is useless," commented Kevin after a long while.

"I have a gut feeling she isn't here. Not here in the woods. At least, not where we are. Darn it, why do girls always have to run away when they have a problem?"

"I don't feel like fighting about this right now," responded Ricki. "But if you're so sure that she isn't here, then maybe you also have a feeling about where she is."

"No, unfortunately not. But let's try to think logically like a girl, if those two words can even be used in the same sentence," Kevin joked, trying to ease the tension. The joke, however, didn't appeal to Ricki.

"You're really a jerk!" she snapped at him, but then she began to think out loud, "Once more. If I were Cheryl, or rather, if I had her problem, then I would ... then I would ..."

"You'd go to Echo Lake and tell the mosquitoes all about it," Kevin finished his girlfriend's sentence.

"That's right!" she confirmed. "And I know exactly where I would go."

"And where's that?" asked Kevin, curious now.

"Think about it logically – and like a guy," Ricki just couldn't help saying, and urged Diablo into a trot. "Come on! I'll show you. You've never been there yourself, I think. It's the most beautiful, secluded, and quiet place along the lake. Gosh, I can't believe I didn't think of it before!"

* * *

Marisa sat with two riding gear catalogs on her lap, which she had skimmed from front to back, again and again. She'd also surfed the Internet countless times looking at riding paraphernalia. If she were to have a horse of her own soon, then she would need a saddle, snaffle, halter, and all sorts of other things.

She wasn't going to have a saddle sent in the mail; she wanted to buy one in person, preferably after she tried it out to make sure it fit her. Still, she was curious to see what was available, and was amazed at how many pages of saddles there were in the catalogs and on the various websites.

"Unbelievable," she murmured to herself, and then she turned to the snaffles and thought about which strap would look best on Sheila.

"Maybe this one with the golden diamond pattern, or maybe the red braided one ..." Finally, Marisa gave up and closed the catalogs. She would have to see Sheila in the flesh before she could pick out her accessories.

Folding her arms beneath her head, she lay back in the big round wicker chair and closed her eyes.

Tomorrow, she thought, her face showing her joy and excitement. *I'm going to see Sheila tomorrow! Wow ... I can hardly believe it! I'm going to have my own horse! MY OWN HORSE! And if everything goes well, I'll be a horse owner by tomorrow night!*

She automatically reached for Sheila's photo, which lay on the little side table next to the chair. She looked at the picture delightedly, and just knew she would love this horse!

* * *

Beth and Logan had taken a detour so they could look for Cheryl, but when they hadn't found her after an hour and a half, they decided to ride toward the Bendix home, and soon they could see the hunting lodge in the distance.

"Welcome home!" said Logan, as he jumped down from the saddle.

"I still can't believe it," beamed Beth, and she led Rondo behind Star into the stable.

The animals looked at their new home full of curiosity, and after the teens had unsaddled them and led them to their stalls, the horses immediately went to their hay-filled racks and began to chew, as though they had never lived anywhere else.

"Isn't that great?" asked Logan as he put his arm around Beth. "They're eating, so they must be happy."

Beth nodded silently.

What a wonderful moment it was, to stand here with her boyfriend and to know that she would feel just as much at home here as Rondo and Star, the two amazing animals that made them so happy.

Silently, the two of them sat down together in a corner, holding hands and watching the horses contentedly munching in their stalls.

"Do you know how glad I am that you and Rondo are here?" asked Logan, and Beth snuggled closer to him.

"Tell me," she answered softly and closed her eyes in order to remember this moment forever.

Just then, however, her cell phone rang, rudely interrupting her state of bliss.

"Oh, no, how mean!" grinned Beth, but when she saw who was calling, she got serious and quickly answered the phone.

"Hey, Cheryl, where are you? Your moth–"

"I just wanted to tell you that I think it's despicable that my best friend arranged for a buyer for my horse!" Cheryl cut in. "That's a horrible thing to do, and I never want to see or speak to you again!" And she hung up without waiting for a response.

"Hey, Cheryl, wait! I ... darn it, she hung up."

Immediately Beth dialed her girlfriend's number so that she could talk with her again, but Cheryl had already turned off her phone.

"That's just unbelievable! What am I going to do now?"

Logan got up and pulled Beth up as well. The romantic mood was gone.

"I think you should call Mrs. Vincent and tell her you heard from Cheryl. Then maybe we could get my mother to drive us over to the ranch and we can tell Carlotta about the phone call.

Beth nodded.

"Yeah, that's probably best." And while Logan ran into the house to get his mother, Beth called Mrs. Vincent. Cheryl's mother was relieved when she heard about the call from her daughter, even though Cheryl still hadn't called home.

"Don't worry, Mrs. Vincent," said Beth, sadly. "If Cheryl is that mad at me, then she's okay!"

* * *

Cheryl was all cried out, and after hours of tears and gloomy thoughts all that was left now was anger. Anger at Beth, by whom she felt betrayed; anger at Carlotta, who obviously didn't care how she felt; anger at her friends, who were lucky enough to own their own horses; and anger at herself, without knowing exactly why.

She got up a little stiffly, and suddenly she knew that she had to ride back. Even if she sat here another ten hours, it wouldn't change the fact that Sheila was going to be sold.

The girl took a few deep breaths to steady herself, glanced one last time at the calming lake, and then had an overwhelming need to flee the wonderful spot. She had been here too long, and the peace suddenly felt oppressive.

Besides, she was starting to feel hungry. After all, she hadn't eaten a thing all day.

How can I be hungry at a time like this? Cheryl asked herself, almost ashamed of the feeling.

Quickly, she pulled her bike out of the bushes and pushed it through the branches and weeds back onto the path that would lead her to the trail through the woods.

She would ride back home now, back to her life, but she was sure that after the hours she had spent here, she would never be the same again.

* * *

Hardly five minutes after Cheryl had left, Ricki and Kevin arrived on their horses.

"Here it is." Ricki stopped Diablo and dismounted.

"Here?" Kevin looked puzzled at the dense bushes. "It's impossible to get through these!"

Ricki laughed.

"Not on horseback, of course, but it's easy on foot. I'm going to go down to the water." She gave her boyfriend Diablo's reins and then she disappeared.

"Bingo!" Kevin heard Ricki shout a few seconds later. Within two minutes, the girl was back. Shaking the leaves out of her hair, she held out a horseshoe-shaped keychain.

"I found this on the shore. It belongs to Cheryl. She must have been here!"

Kevin nodded admiringly.

"It's too bad you didn't think of this spot a little sooner. Maybe we'd have caught up with her then."

"Yeah, that's just what I was thinking. But there's no sense looking any more. We should ride back home."

Just then, Kevin got a text message: *Didn't find her. We're riding home. Lillian*

"Okay, then let's go. Since we didn't find Cheryl, I think it's okay if we don't call her mother until we get home. What do you think?"

"I agree. And we can start thinking about how to tell her that we weren't successful."

Ricki sighed. To be honest, she hoped that Kevin would make that call.

* * *

Beth and Logan had to bike to Mercy Ranch, because Mr. Bendix's car was in the service station and Logan's mother had to pick up her husband at work. When they arrived, they found Rondo's and Star's stalls were already clean.

"Oh, Carlotta, you shouldn't have cleaned up. We told you we were going to do that!" Beth scolded.

"You can help me another time," she responded. "I need the exercise! Oh, by the way, did I tell you that your cousin is coming tomorrow to look at Sheila?"

"No. Really? When? Then I'll come here, too. I haven't seen her in ages!" Beth was very excited about seeing Marisa again.

"Your relatives are going to try to be here at three o'clock."

"Oh, terrific! That'll work! Logan, you'll come too, won't you?" Beth turned to look at her boyfriend.

"If nothing happens in the meantime, sure," he replied, and then he turned to Carlotta. "Then we can help out in the stalls tomorrow."

The older woman laughed. "Great! I won't say no to that."

"Do you think Ricki and the others are coming by today? They meant to, but since they haven't arrived yet, maybe they're not coming."

"I think you're right. It's probably better if you go home, too. You both have a pretty long bike ride."

"Oh, that's true. And I'm so tired today, what with moving the horses and this thing with Cheryl." Beth made a face.

"Let's wait a bit. I'm almost sure she's home by now. If not I think Mrs. Vincent would have called me to ask if she had turned up here at the ranch."

"Yeah, probably, but she was so furious at me because of Marisa."

Carlotta put her hand on Beth's shoulder.

"Believe me, that will work out, too. Eventually she'll be grateful to you, when she realizes that Sheila has found a good home. And if I know Cheryl, she'll put Sheila's happiness before her own. I don't think she'll be mad at you for long. You two are best friends after all, and deep down she knows that you didn't want to hurt her. You just wanted the best for Sheila."

"I hope you're right, Carlotta ... But now I'd better get our gear."

Beth ran over to the tack room to get Logan's and her grooming kits and then she ran over and gave Carlotta a hug.

"See you tomorrow! Say hello to Marisa for me if she gets here before we do."

"I will! Bye, you two. Have a safe trip home."

Lillian and Cathy were back at the Sulais' stable before Ricki and Kevin, and were waiting impatiently for them to arrive.

"There's news!" Lillian called out from the entrance to the stable, when she saw them coming.

"Good news or bad news?" asked Kevin.

"Good news. Cheryl is home. Her mother called and told me. She thanked us for looking for her."

"That's great! I'm so glad." Ricki was relieved. "I was dreading facing Mrs. Vincent," she admitted.

"Why? She's not ugly!" Kevin was already joking.

"Idiot! You know what I meant."

"We'll see who's an idiot. Tell me, how did you do on the math test? We haven't talked about it yet."

"I don't feel like talking about it right now. I'd rather just take back 'idiot'!" groaned Ricki, and Kevin let her off the hook.

"Okay!"

Suddenly Jake was standing in the doorway.

"If you leave your grooming equipment lying around in the corridor again when you go riding, I'm really going to get angry!" he said, looking at them accusingly.

"This is all we need," mumbled Cathy.

"It was an emergency, Jake! Cheryl disappeared and we went looking for her. We had to hurry and we didn't want to lose any time."

"And? Did you find her?" the old man wanted to know.

"No, unfortunately. But she's back home now."

Jake stared at Ricki, his expression angry.

"You couldn't think of any other alibi, huh?" Then he saw the grass stains on Holli.

"And you don't think you need to clean your horse before you saddle him, do you?" he chastised Lillian, who couldn't help turning bright red.

"As I said, it was an emergency, because of Cheryl." replied Ricki, defending her friends.

"You kids think I'm a stupid old man, don't you?" Jake thought they were making fun of him, especially since Kevin and Cathy were trying not to laugh. The old man stomped outside, feeling insulted.

"Disappeared!" he mumbled to himself. "Ridiculous!"

* * *

Cheryl stood in front of her mother, miserable, when Andrea Vincent opened the door.

"Do you know how worried I've been?" Mrs. Vincent asked. She wanted to be angry, but she was so relieved that Cheryl was home safe that she hugged her daughter close and then cupped her face in her hands.

"I'm so glad you're back. Your friends looked for you all day on horseback, and I almost went crazy worrying about you."

"Oh, Mom, I'm really sorry," stammered Cheryl. Her anger was spent and now all she felt was empty and exhausted. She was so sleepy that she didn't even feel hungry anymore. All she wanted was to go to bed.

"I'm so tired," she said softly, barely able to keep her eyes open.

Although her mother was dying to know where she had been all day, she smoothed her daughter's hair and said, "Go to bed, Cheryl; you'll feel better in the morning. We'll talk about everything tomorrow, when you get back from school, okay?"

Cheryl nodded sleepily. She was really grateful to her mother for not making a scene when she returned home. She walked to her room, her shoulders hanging with fatigue, collapsed onto her bed, and fell asleep almost instantly.

"Poor dear!" Andrea Vincent whispered about a half an hour later, when she went to look in on her daughter. Lovingly she pulled up the blanket and then left the room on tiptoe, thankful that Cheryl was home.

Chapter 7

Cheryl joined the kids at lunch the next day. At first she was a little embarrassed because she knew she had upset them by disappearing the day before. However, when she noticed that no one was saying anything to her about it, and they were also avoiding any discussions having to do with Sheila, she felt greatly relieved and was able to relax. She backed off only when Beth arrived, and then she purposely walked off in the other direction.

"Uh-oh, it looks as though she's still mad at me." Beth announced sadly. It really hurt her that her friend didn't seem to want to have anything to do with her.

"Give her a little time to deal with Sheila being sold. She'll be back when she's dealt with that. She'll get over it," said Ricki.

"That's what Carlotta said, too." Beth looked over at Cheryl and lowered her voice. "By the way, my cousin's coming to the ranch this afternoon to take a look at Sheila."

"Really? When?" Ricki wanted to know.

"About three o'clock. Logan and I want to go, too ... Oh, guys, you wouldn't believe how totally happy Rondo and Star are in the new stable!" Beth slid from one topic to another, and while she was telling her friends how the animals felt right at home on their first day together, Cheryl walked back to her classroom.

Today, already! she thought, her stomach cramping when she overheard Beth mention her cousin's visit. *She's coming this afternoon! That means if all goes well, today is the last chance I'll have to see Sheila.* Cheryl sat down at her desk and stared at the blackboard, as though the solution to her problem was written there.

I have to go out to the ranch one more time, she thought. *I have to say good-bye to Sheila!* Cheryl forced herself not to cry. She knew that her classmates would gossip about her if they saw tears in her eyes.

Marisa was so excited, it was hard for her to sit through school that morning, and now she was doing her homework in her room, hardly able to think straight. In one hour she and her parents would be on their way to see Sheila.

This darn French! she thought, struggling with the translation. Normally she found French to be easy, but today, for obvious reasons, she just couldn't concentrate. It was a shame that her mother insisted she do her homework before starting off to Mercy Ranch. Surely she would have time for that in the evening.

"If it works out with the horse, you'll feel even less like doing schoolwork tonight!" Mona had said, and finally Marisa gave in.

"Finished!" she exhaled thirty minutes later, and then she slammed her French book and her notebook shut and stuffed them in her backpack. Now she was glad her mother had made her do it all, because she could concentrate on Sheila.

"As far as I'm concerned, we can leave now," she called out two minutes later in the kitchen and looked at her parents with shining eyes.

Patrick glanced at his watch and nodded.

"All right! Then get your riding clothes on. I imagine you'd like to ride the horse and try her out."

"Yeah!" Marisa took off like a shot.

"We're going to get there a little early," Mona said to Patrick, but he just laughed.

"I'd rather get there a little early than have Marisa drive us crazy before we even get started."

* * *

After school, Kevin and Ricki brought their horses in from the paddock to get them ready for a ride. Lillian and Cathy didn't have time to go to the Sulais' stable that afternoon, so Doc Holliday and Rashid would have to stay on the paddock and relax with Chico and Salina.

"What would you say to a ride to Mercy Ranch to have a look at Beth's cousin? I'm curious to see who's going to get Sheila." Ricki swung herself up into Diablo's saddle.

"Sure, why not!" Kevin steered Sharazan over to the black horse and they rode out of the Sulais' yard.

"Hey, Lillian and I had a brilliant idea yesterday," Ricki began as they walked their horses along. "It's about that Fun and Games Festival."

Kevin groaned loudly. "Oh, no. Not again!"

"Just listen for a minute. We thought that since you weren't having any fun anyway, maybe you could let Cheryl use Sharazan."

"What?"

"Well, we wanted to ask Cheryl if she'd be interested in participating in the tournament, but if Sheila is sold she won't have a horse to ride. So, if you don't feel like taking part in the games, maybe Cheryl could participate on Sharazan, assuming that it's all right with you and she's still interested in riding after Sheila's gone." Ricki looked hopefully at her boyfriend. At first he didn't say anything.

"What do you think?" she asked again, and Kevin shrugged his shoulders.

"Well, I don't know ... I don't like other people riding my horse."

"But Cheryl rides really well, you know that!"

"I know, but would you let someone else ride Diablo?"

Now Ricki was quiet.

After thinking about it, she had to admit that she wouldn't have been so happy about it herself. Actually, she wouldn't have liked it at all. How had she imagined that Kevin would be excited about the idea?

"Okay, forget about it."

"I didn't say that I was totally against it, I just have to think about it some more. You haven't talked to Cheryl about it yet, have you?"

"No, of course not. And it's not a problem if she can't ride Sharazan because Lillian has already offered to let her ride Holli. Then his name would be announced twice, that's all."

"I'll think about it," Kevin promised, and after just a few minutes he had a mischievous look on his face. "I would love it if Sharazan shot by all the obstacles with Cheryl, instead of doing the slalom, and then I could claim that I would have done much better!"

Ricki laughed heartily. "I knew it would be more fun for you to make someone else look ridiculous!"

"I won't answer that without my lawyer." Kevin grinned back at her, then the two of them shortened the reins and allowed their horses to break into a light gallop.

* * *

Carlotta stood at the entrance to her stable and looked toward the paddock, where all the Mercy Ranch horses were enjoying the sunny day. Soon Beth's cousin would arrive with her parents, and Carlotta thought about bringing Sheila in, but then she decided not to.

Who knows, maybe they won't like her at all, and then the animal will have missed two wonderful hours on the paddock for no good reason, she thought. *And if Sheila does appeal to Marisa, and the two get along well, then it wouldn't be a bad idea for the girl to clean her herself and maybe saddle her, to try her out.*

Automatically Carlotta's thoughts switched to Cheryl. She wondered how she was feeling right now, and whether she had begun to deal with the situation a little better. Or was she still crying her eyes out?

Carlotta cared a lot about the kids who went in and out of the ranch every day, and she was especially sad when she had to disappoint one of them. If it had been possible for Cheryl to pay for Sheila's upkeep, Carlotta wouldn't have hesitated giving her the horse. She knew that the horse would have been well taken care of. Sheila and Cheryl were perfect together.

She sighed and went back into the stable. She would be so glad when this whole thing was over.

* * *

Cheryl had gone home immediately after school, prepared to explain the previous day's disappearance to her mother. When she got there, however, she found a note on the kitchen table.

Cheryl hon,
I have to work this afternoon. One of my colleagues is out sick, and I'm not sure when I'll be home. Your dinner is in the refrigerator. Please be home by 8 p.m., at the latest.
Love, Mom

Cheryl sighed with relief. She hoped that her mother would be too tired after working at the hospital to talk to her about yesterday.

Cheryl opened the refrigerator and glanced at a plate of sliced meatloaf, mashed sweet potato, and some green beans. Although she was hungry, she was way too nervous to eat anything.

If she started her homework right away, she could be done in time to be at the ranch by 3:30.

The girl started to think it over. Would she really be able to be near Beth's cousin? Would she be able to bear seeing a happy gleam in Marisa's eyes, knowing that Marisa was going to take Sheila home with her?

Cheryl let herself fall heavily into a kitchen chair.

No! I can't do it! she thought, but then she changed her mind and decided that she would hide somewhere on the ranch and sneak a peek at the new owner. Maybe she would get the chance to go over to Sheila one more time when no one was watching, and say good-bye to her without anyone knowing. Yes, that's what she was going to do!

* * *

Beth parked her bike in front of the Bendixes' lodge and was just about to ring the doorbell when she heard Logan's voice.

"I'm over here!" he called from the stable and waved a pitchfork happily.

"Hey!" Beth responded and ran over to him. "I hurried so that we could get started on time."

Logan gave her a hug.

"I'm glad you're here. But listen, I just let the horses out onto the paddock so they could get to know it. It wouldn't be a good idea to take them back in right away. It's best if we leave them in the paddock in peace for today."

Beth was disappointed. "Oh, but I was looking forward to riding over to the ranch."

"We can ride over on our bikes. It's just that I think it's better if the animals get used to their new surroundings today."

Beth nodded.

"I guess you're right. Still, I really wanted to show Marisa Rondo ... Oh well, whatever." She looked at her watch.

"If we want to get there on time, then we have to leave right now, or else they may leave before we get there."

Logan laughed.

"I'm sure they'll still be there. You need time to check out a horse that you might want to buy. A lot! You need more than just half an hour. So don't worry, you'll still get to see your cousin. By the way, I've already finished cleaning the stalls. That means we can leave any time."

Beth beamed.

"Terrific! But tomorrow it's my turn to muck out the stalls," she said with a determined tone of voice.

Logan grinned.

"Don't worry! You'll have plenty of opportunities for that."

He quickly parked the wheelbarrow to the side and put the pitchfork back in its place.

"Done! Let's get going," he said as he brushed the dust off his jeans and got his bike out of the garage. In less than a minute, the two teens were on their way to Carlotta's.

* * *

"It's really beautiful here!" Marisa called out excitedly as Patrick steered their car into the driveway of Mercy Ranch. "And there's the paddock over there. I wonder if Sheila is there with the other horses?"

Excitedly, she pressed her nose flat against the window.

"She is! The horse to the left of the gray one, that could be Sheila! Wow, if it is, she's even more beautiful than the photo that Beth sent me."

Carlotta saw the approaching car and came outside, leaning on her crutch.

After Marisa and her parents had gotten out of the car and exchanged polite pleasantries, Carlotta knew she hadn't been wrong about her first impression on the phone. They seemed like very nice people.

She turned to Marisa, who had been glancing over at the paddock.

"So, let's go over to meet Sheila. You probably can't wait, can you?" She smiled as Marisa nodded vigorously.

"Is that Sheila, over there on the paddock?" the girl asked hopefully.

"Yes!" Carlotta took the lead, and without even looking back, she knew that Marisa's face was all smiles.

When they had arrived at the paddock fence, the horses' heads all flew up and there were several whinnied greetings as the animals recognized Carlotta.

Mercy Ranch's owner told Marisa and her parents briefly about Sheila's previous life, and didn't forget to mention how horribly the previous owners had treated her.

"It took a while before Sheila could trust people again, but now we have no problems with her at all. She is affectionate and gentle, unproblematic as far as the blacksmith is concerned, and easy to ride. Cheryl, who took very good care of her, is fourteen and she took her trail riding almost every day."

"How old is Sheila?" Marisa wanted to know.

"She's a good ten years old and completely healthy. You're welcome to have a vet come and examine her before you buy her if you'd like," offered Carlotta, looking at Marisa's parents.

For a while the potential buyers stood there silently and watched the herd of horses. Marisa's glance hung on the beautiful Black Forest Shire mare, while Mona pointed out the somewhat larger gray horse to her husband.

"He's nice, too. What's his name?"

"That's Silver. He's eleven years old and his previous owner got rid of him because he was no longer good enough for tournaments. He has some joint problems because he was trained too early and forced into jumping too young. But, I have to say, it's only a problem when he's overstressed. Normally, and when he isn't forced to do extremely long rides or jumps, there are no problems."

"Ah!" Mona had listened closely, not admitting that she actually didn't know anything about horses.

Marisa had also listened carefully to Carlotta's words, and she thought that her mother was absolutely right. Silver appealed to her as well. While Sheila had gone back to grazing the delicious grass, the gray horse kept looking over at her.

"Come," Carlotta said suddenly to Marisa. "Let's go onto the paddock and get Sheila. After all, you want to get to know her better, don't you?"

"Absolutely," the girl replied, reining in her desire to run to the paddock, and instead followed Carlotta, who bent down somewhat awkwardly to get through the fence rails.

Together they walked slowly toward the horses, who came toward them immediately, obviously hoping that Carlotta had a few treats in her pocket.

The animals pushed in close and, laughing, Carlotta nudged their heads away.

"Greedy bunch!" she scolded and winked at Marisa.

Silver pushed closer to Marisa and touched her hands with his velvety nose. Then, a little fresh, he blew warm air onto her face.

Spontaneously, she wrapped her arms around the animal's beautiful head.

"You're really sweet! It's too bad you're not for sale!" She glanced over at Carlotta. "To be honest, I like him even better than Sheila."

"Oh, yes?" Carlotta nodded at her. "Silver is a wonderful horse! Nothing upsets him, but unfortunately, as I said, he's not completely healthy. That's why I think you would be happier with Sheila, and I'm almost certain you'll fall for her charm. Up to now, every rider has fallen in love with her!" Carlotta reached for the mare's halter.

"Come, lady, it's time!" she said, and led her away from the other horses easily, while Marisa, once again, and almost sadly, patted Silver's neck before following Carlotta and turning her attention to Sheila. After all, she had come here expressly to look at this horse.

"Can I take her?" asked Marisa, earnestly.

"Of course! But be careful. Sometimes she's such a klutz that she steps on your feet."

"If that's all, that's nothing," laughed the girl and took the rope. Marisa led Sheila across the paddock and proudly past Mona and Patrick, then toward the stable, as if she had done this many times before. She already felt as though Sheila belonged to her.

"Tie her onto that ring over there in front of the third stall on the right. I'll bring you a grooming kit and then you can spend some time with her and give Sheila the opportunity to get to know you, too," said Carlotta, and then left for the tack room. When she returned, she handed Marisa a rubber brush, a currycomb, a soft brush, and the hoof scraper.

"And don't worry, she's very gentle."

Marisa smiled at the ranch owner.

"I'm not scared."

"Well, then that's fine."

"Can I ride her afterward for a while?" Marisa looked expectantly at Carlotta.

"Of course. After all, you have to decide if she's right for you," Carlotta said and turned to Marisa's parents, "assuming you have no objections to a trial ride. I have to add that it would be completely your responsibility, and I have to ask you to sign a form that states just that."

Patrick hesitated.

"I thought the horse was so gentle?" he asked a little suspiciously.

"She is! But you have to understand that I don't want to take any risks."

"Hmmm ... okay."

While Carlotta went to fetch the form from the office, Marisa talked with her parents.

"Do you like her?" Mona wanted to know.

"Yes! She's really sweet! I'm dying to see how she is to ride," the girl said excitedly, as she brushed the horse's soft coat.

"Be careful when you mount her. The animal doesn't know you yet," warned Patrick, but Marisa just laughed.

"I'm sure Sheila wouldn't hurt a flea," she said, completely convinced. Carlotta was back and she handed Patrick the form and a pen to sign with.

For a moment Marisa's father hesitated, but then he signed with a flourish.

"Thank you very much." Carlotta folded the paper and put it in her pocket without paying much attention. She knew that it was just a formality. All of her animals were extremely reliable.

She watched Marisa as the girl approached Sheila with confidence. She could tell that Marisa had spent a lot of time around horses.

A good beginning, thought Carlotta. *I like this girl!*

* * *

Cheryl rode her bike up close to the ranch and leaned it against a tree. She hid behind a large bush near the small riding ring and watched Marisa from her hiding place.

When she saw Marisa take Sheila from Carlotta on the paddock and lead her into the stable, she bit her knuckles to keep from crying. She couldn't hear anything for quite a while afterward, and wondered if they were already signing the papers for Sheila. The thought drove Cheryl almost crazy with grief.

She wanted to run into the stable and scream at those people that Sheila was a very mean horse and hard to ride, so they wouldn't want to buy her. But she couldn't lie like that. She couldn't do that to Sheila or to Carlotta, and so Cheryl waited, crouched behind the bush. The people hadn't brought a horse trailer with them. That meant that if they bought Sheila they would have to come again, and that meant she would have time to say good-bye to her darling horse.

Marisa suddenly appeared with Sheila, saddled, in the stable doorway, followed by Carlotta and the two other adults.

Cheryl was startled and she held her breath.

Oh, my sweet, why did you let her saddle you? She was almost angry with herself for teaching the animal to stand still while she was being saddled.

"Over there is a little riding ring," called Carlotta, and pointed in Cheryl's direction. She drew herself in as much as she could so she wouldn't be seen.

Marisa nodded and led Sheila into the fenced area, while Carlotta closed it in with two poles.

"To start, let her walk around a few times with the reins long, before you try any figures or pace changes with her," the ranch owner instructed. Then Marisa tightened the girth with shaking hands, adjusted the length of the stirrups, patted Sheila on the neck, and mounted.

Contrary to her usual calm, the girl was pretty nervous, and this feeling transferred to the horse immediately. When Marisa put her foot in the stirrup, Sheila turned around completely.

"Brrr ... stop ... stand still," Marisa tried to calm the animal, and when Sheila was still, she tried again, but the horse was upset and threw up her head, her ears down.

"Good, Sheila! Show her that you're not right for her!" hissed Cheryl through her teeth. She clenched her fists so tightly that the joints of her fingers turned white.

A little embarrassed and a little uncertain, Marisa glanced at Carlotta, who was hurrying toward her.

Resolutely, she grabbed the reins. "Stand still, Sheila!" she said very clearly, and the horse obeyed immediately, so that the girl could finally mount her.

"You're too nervous right now, my dear." Carlotta smiled at Marisa understandingly. "Sheila is very sensitive and feels that immediately."

"I'm sorry, I don't know what's wrong," replied Marisa embarrassed.

"You don't have to be sorry, but try to calm down, and then be very clear with your aids, so that Sheila knows exactly what you want. She's used to being able to rely on her rider, and if you're unsure of yourself, you'll make her nervous, and I don't have to tell you what that means. You've been riding long enough to know horses, haven't you?"

Marisa had turned bright red and was mad at herself, but she nodded. She knew that she was a good rider, but the fact that this trial ride would determine if she would own this wonderful horse made her so nervous she could hardly control herself.

"All right!" said Carlotta encouragingly. She slapped Sheila lightly on the croup.

Marisa took another deep breath, and then she pressed her calves lightly on the horse's belly and left the reins long as she guided her along. In the beginning she was still nervous, but then, after a few rounds, the girl got her confidence back. Soon she tightened the reins a bit and tried to change the pace into a trot.

Sheila was great to ride and Marisa almost felt as though she were on a cloud.

Fabulous! Marisa thought, delighted. *I could trot like this forever!* After a while she did a few figures, slowed the horse down, had her step backward, and then, finally, she let Sheila gallop and the animal arched her neck magnificently.

* * *

Cheryl couldn't stop her tears now. As she sobbed quietly, she turned herself around, burst out from behind the bush, and ran over to her bike. She could no longer bear to watch Sheila and her rider, especially since she had to admit that Marisa rode much better than she did. She pedaled away furiously, wishing that she were home already. She was sure she had lost Sheila forever.

* * *

Marisa had been riding for about half an hour when Ricki and Kevin arrived at Mercy Ranch on their horses.

"Hey, look!" Ricki pointed at the riding ring. "She's doing really well!"

Kevin looked over, too, and nodded in agreement.

"Yes, Beth's cousin looks great in the saddle."

Ricki grinned.

"I was talking about the horse, not the girl!"

Slowly, they rode Diablo and Sharazan over to Carlotta and Marisa's parents and came to a halt in front of them.

"Hey," the kids greeted them casually.

"How's it going?" asked Ricki, still watching Sheila with fascination.

"Hello, you two! It's going well, as you can see. It looks as though the two of them like each other," Carlotta winked at Kevin, as he slid down from Sharazan's saddle.

"This is really amazing!" called out Marisa, a little out of breath, as she rode over to them. "She's wonderful to ride!" She jumped down from the saddle and patted Sheila's neck enthusiastically, but she couldn't avoid glancing over at Silver, who was still watching her intently.

I wonder if he's as good to ride? Marisa asked herself, but then she shook off those thoughts. Carlotta had said absolutely nothing about whether she would sell Silver. Even though Marisa had always preferred Black Forest Shire horses, she had to admit that she felt more drawn to the gray gelding than to Sheila, although Sheila was so gentle and wonderful to ride.

Hey, Marisa, don't be ungrateful, the girl scolded herself. After thinking about it for a bit, she was pretty sure that she was going to love Sheila when the horse actually belonged to her.

Carlotta opened the poles so that the girl could leave the ring on the horse.

Mona and Patrick looked at each other.

"Do you think you want this horse?" Patrick asked his daughter.

For a second, Marisa hesitated, but then she nodded decisively.

"Absolutely! But still, I'd like to go for a ride with her. Would that be okay?"

Carlotta nodded. "Why not? But please, stay in sight."

"Of course! I'd just like to ride down that path, and try a short gallop, and then I'll come right back!" Marisa promised. She led Sheila a few steps off in order to remount, but although the girl was no longer nervous, the mare began to shy and tried to stop her from getting into the saddle again. It seemed as if she realized that this ride would determine whether or not she was going to stay at Mercy Ranch!

Chapter 8

"Huh, what's going on?" Kevin was puzzled as he watched Sheila's sudden change in behavior. "She isn't usually like that. Did she act like that before we came?"

"Just for a little bit, but then she calmed down." Carlotta couldn't explain either why the horse was acting so erratic all of a sudden.

Marisa tried to remount, and then Sheila drew up her left leg almost to her belly and kicked hard several times, just barely past the girl, who managed to get her foot out of the stirrup and jump to the side just in time.

The sudden movement startled Sheila, and she tore the reins out of Marisa's hand and raced straight across the yard toward freedom.

"Sheila!" shouted Carlotta and limped a few steps after the horse. "Sheila! Come back here right now!"

With a sudden burst of speed, Diablo galloped past her. Reacting quickly, Ricki had started after Sheila, followed by Kevin, who jumped into the saddle and raced after her.

They both knew it would be terrible for Sheila to get her legs tangled in the reins at that speed.

"I'm not hurt!" Marisa calmed her worried parents. Patrick turned to Carlotta rather upset.

"So that's the one-hundred-percent reliable horse you were talking about?" he asked, his voice tinged with anger and his face pale with concern for his daughter's safety. "I knew there was a reason why I had to sign that form before Marisa got into that saddle!"

Carlotta shook her head vigorously. "Oh, no, Mr. Swinton. I can't let you believe that! There are so many young people who are in and out of here all the time, who are with the horses every day and ride regularly. It would be an enormous risk for me to allow them to handle violent horses. Sheila *is* reliable, and I have no idea what's gotten into her. Marisa, could you have pushed the toe of your boot into her belly as you were mounting?"

The girl looked at her bewildered.

"I ... hmm ... have no idea! Not that I know of, but of course, it's possible."

"Mrs. Mancini, don't try to blame my daughter!"

Carlotta wasn't even listening to what Patrick was saying. She was watching Ricki and Kevin as they rode off at top speed.

Sheila had galloped past the paddock and was now heading toward the road that ran in front of the ranch. Diablo was at her heels, but the more she felt the black horse behind her, the faster Sheila ran.

Ricki knew she could never catch Sheila. She looked around and saw Kevin behind her.

"Go right and I'll go left," Kevin shouted at her. They

immediately steered their horses away from Sheila so she wouldn't feel as though she were being chased.

"Run, Diablo!" Ricki urged her horse on. "Run, run, run! Come on!" and the black horse caught up, one yard after another. Ricki stared straight ahead.

"Oh, no, the road! THE ROAD! SHEILAAAAAAA! Oh, NOOO!" Ricki screamed. With all her strength she managed to halt Diablo just as she saw the approaching truck, and Kevin brought Sharazan to a sliding stop, as well as any western rider could have managed.

"Noooooo!" screamed Ricki loudly and closed her eyes so that she wouldn't see what happened next.

Sheila raced and slid over the road; she almost fell but then regained her balance and escaped the honking truck by mere inches.

The truck, with a wildly gesticulating driver, had barely passed when Ricki and Kevin took up the chase again.

"She's gone wild!" yelled Kevin. "We have to try to cut her off!"

Good idea, thought Ricki, but she had no idea how they were going to do it. *It will be a miracle if we catch her, and it's just a matter of time until the next car or truck drives by!*

* * *

"Darn bike!" said Beth with great annoyance. "We should have ridden the horses. At least they don't get flat tires." She kept looking at her watch. "I'm starting to think I won't get to see Marisa after all." Resigned, she looked at Logan, who was kneeling in front of her upturned bike trying to patch the tire.

"Oh, don't worry, I'm almost finished," he said comfortingly.

"You've been saying that for at least fifteen minutes!" replied Beth.

"I don't have much practice," the volunteer bike mechanic defended himself. Suddenly he felt a knock on his back.

"Hey, are you crazy? What –?"

Beth pointed excitedly in one direction.

"Look over there! That's ... There's a horse without a rider and ... Oh, no ... there's Diablo and Sharazan! And that's –"

"Sheila! That's Sheila! Good grief, what happened? I hope your cousin didn't fall off while she was trying her out!" Logan burst out. He jumped up and threw the bike aside.

"You think Marisa is lying hurt somewhere?" Beth turned pale. She stared at the racing mare, gripped with worry.

"She's coming right toward us!" Logan stared at the animal, and then he grabbed Beth's arm and pulled her with him. "Come on! Maybe we can stop her!" They ran toward the horse and hoped that Sheila would stay on course and not make any turns.

* * *

Cheryl was back home, happy that she was alone in the apartment.

Sad and distracted, she drank a big glass of milk before going to her room, where photos of Sheila lay all over the floor.

Mechanically, the girl bent down and started to pick them up, one after the other. Then she sat at her desk, lit a candle and picked up a pair of scissors.

She looked at each photo for a long time, and then she cut them all into tiny pieces. She didn't want to keep anything that would remind her of Sheila. It would hurt too much to remember the wonderful times they had spent together. Cheryl knew that if she didn't destroy the photos, she would look at them every day and feel miserable.

With tears in her eyes, she looked at her favorite photo for the last time. It showed her with Sheila and, for a moment, she was tempted to keep at least this one, but then she cut it up just like all the others.

Exhausted, she dropped the scissors and shoved the snips of paper into the wastebasket. Then she grabbed a sheet of her horse stationery and, after staring at the candle flame for a long time, she began to write ...

In the Valley of Tears
In the valley of tears
Imprisoned forever,
I cry for the happiness
That was stolen from me.
Robbed of everything
That was important to me,
Without asking,
How I am,
Without seeing
That my heart is broken,
Without feeling
What I have lost.
In the valley of tears,
Imprisoned forever,

My heart bleeds
And I wait for a miracle.
I wait
And wait
And wait,
Although I know
That this miracle
Will never happen,
Because
What I lost,
Will never again
Come back to me.
Nevertheless,
I'll keep waiting
In the hope
That one day
My tears will stop,
That one day
My heart will laugh again
And I will be able
To free myself
From the valley of tears
So that I can rise up
To a new happiness,
Whenever that will be.
At the moment, I can't believe in it,
Because my heart and my thoughts
Will always be with you, Sheila.

Cheryl dropped her pen and buried her face in her arms, overcome with sadness. A life without Sheila? The thought of it seemed awful to her. She would never have believed this could hurt so much.

* * *

"I am convinced that THAT is not the right horse for our daughter!" said Patrick Swinton emphatically to Carlotta. He was still upset by Sheila's behavior, and Marisa could already see "her own horse" disappearing.

"Dad, please, maybe it really was my fault," interrupted Marisa, desperate. She was very worried about Sheila.

"We'll find another horse for you," her father said decisively.

"But ..."

"No buts!" Patrick firmly shook his head, and then he looked at Mona, who nodded, still somewhat pale.

"I can understand how you feel," murmured Carlotta distractedly, staring in the direction of the road, where Sheila, with Diablo and Sharazan following on her heels, had long since disappeared behind the trees. She was filled with worry for the horse, leaving no room to think or talk about Sheila's behavior.

Marisa pressed her hands against her stomach. She was feeling nauseated as a result of all the excitement.

"I'm so sorry!" she said again and again softly. "I didn't want this to happen."

"Nor I!" Carlotta managed a sad smile.

"I'll never forgive myself if something happens to Sheila," added Marisa, but Carlotta just held up her hand wearily.

"At the moment we can only hope that Ricki and Kevin stop her in time. If not, then ..." Carlotta left the sentence incomplete and the entire Swinton family could feel what was in her heart.

"Can we do anything?" asked Mona after a few seconds of silence.

"I don't know what you could do."

"Couldn't we get in the car and look for Sheila? It's so awful just standing here, not knowing what's happening to her." Marisa looked at her parents pleadingly.

Patrick nodded.

"Okay. Would you like to come with us, Mrs. Mancini?" Carlotta shook her head.

"No, when Ricki and Kevin come back I'd like to be here, but I do appreciate your help. Thank you."

Mona put her hand on Carlotta's shoulder comfortingly.

"It's the least we can do. After all, if we hadn't been here it never would have happened." Then she turned away, and ran to the car, where Patrick and Marisa were waiting. The car quickly zoomed off toward the road.

"Please, let all of them get back safe and sound: Ricki, Kevin, and Sheila," whispered Carlotta, as she rubbed her hand across her eyes.

* * *

Marisa sat in the backseat of the car and stared out the window. She had come to Mercy Ranch so full of hope, and now she was so unhappy. She felt responsible for what had happened, and her fears for Sheila grew and grew.

Marisa shook her head. All of a sudden she wasn't so sure that she wanted her own horse. If only Sheila would be okay ...

* * *

From a distance, Kevin and Ricki saw two people standing a little apart, obviously putting themselves deliberately in Sheila's way.

The riders knew they would have to try to keep Sheila from changing direction, and they also would need to have their horses ride past her at the perfect spot and then halt behind the two people to cut Sheila off. They hoped this would cause her to stop, but at the moment, with Sheila still so far ahead, it seemed impossible.

Ricki and Kevin exchanged glances and knew they were both thinking the same thing. They loosened the reins and their horses stretched themselves out more with each gallop, so that Ricki felt that Diablo was becoming thinner and longer.

She bent way over his neck, as the black horse raced dangerously fast over the meadow.

Ricki loved a fast gallop more than anything, but at this speed she wasn't so sure of herself. She didn't dare think of what would happen if Diablo stumbled or stepped into a hole.

Sheila's strength seemed to be giving out a little, although the two geldings chased her without slowing down. They got closer and closer to the mare, but they would have to be even faster to overtake her.

"Come on, boy, you can do it!" Ricki shouted into her horse's ears and tried to shut out her own fear of this crazy ride.

Diablo's neck was covered in sweat and Ricki was afraid that sooner or later the leather reins would slip out of her hands. She clenched her fingers holding the reins around his mane and felt her muscles tighten.

"Come, on, come on, Ricki! We almost have her! We have to go past her! Can you hear me? Go past her!" Kevin screamed over to her.

The girl swallowed her fear.

"Okay, let's go! Diablo! Run as fast as you can! Run! RUN!" And Diablo did his best.

* * *

"Oh, no!" Beth stared with disbelief at the thundering horses racing toward her, and was tempted to turn and run away as fast as she could, but Logan stood like a rock and slowly stretched out his arms.

"Don't be afraid! A horse would never run over a person! Do you hear me? Never!" he called to her, seeming to sense her apprehension.

I hope the horse knows that, Beth thought. Then she stretched out her arms as well and forced herself to stand still.

Sheila came closer and closer, and suddenly Diablo and Sharazan were beside her, preventing her from turning.

Kevin tried to grab Sheila's reins, but he couldn't reach them, and he had to be careful not to fall out of the saddle.

Beth's eyes grew larger and larger. As the horses came straight at her, she was more afraid than she had ever been in her life.

"Oh no, oh no, oh no, oh –" she whispered tonelessly to herself, but then she got her voice under control.

"Whoa-whoaaaa, Sheila, Sheilaaaaaaa, brrrrrrr, stoppp, brrrrrrrrr ..." she called out, and was surprised to hear how calm her voice sounded.

The horses were close, and then, as if on command, Diablo and Sharazan rushed past Sheila first, and then past Logan and Beth.

Ricki and Kevin stopped their horses short a few yards away and put them in Sheila's path. The mare would have to slow down if she wanted to get by them, and that would be the moment when perhaps they could finally catch her.

"Whoaaaa, Sheila, whoaaaa," shouted Logan and Beth in unison, and the mare, completely confused by Diablo, Sharazan, and the people waving their arms, lost her stride and stumbled just in front of Beth.

"Grab her, Beth! Go on, hurry!" shouted Logan, and he ran, but his girlfriend had already reached the stumbling horse and grabbed the reins before Sheila could get back on her feet.

"Calm down, sweetie! Everything's okay!" said Beth, her voice shaking and her knees wobbly. Shivering, she stroked Sheila's sweaty neck and was more than glad when Logan took the reins out of her hands soon after.

"Hey, you did that really well! Awesome!" he smiled at his girlfriend.

"Wow, it was really lucky you guys happened to be here. That could have been a complete disaster." Kevin nodded his thanks to the two of them and then looked over at Ricki, who was sitting in the saddle, as white as a ghost.

"Everything okay?" he asked, worried.

"Uh-huh," the girl barely managed to reply, and nodded weakly.

Carefully Ricki unclenched her fingers, then opened and closed them slowly, letting movement return.

"I thought I was going to die on that gallop," she said softly and looked down at her black horse in wonder. "I always knew that he was fast, but I didn't know he was a racehorse. I've never been so scared!"

Kevin grinned. He felt exactly the same, but he was never going to admit that to his girlfriend.

"Is Sheila okay?" he asked Logan, who was trying to calm the excited, snorting mare.

"I think so. What happened?"

"It was just a bad situation," began Ricki, slowly getting her voice back. Then she told them what had happened at Mercy Ranch.

"Wow, Carlotta is sure lucky you were there!" Beth looked at the two of them anxiously. "And is everything okay with Marisa?"

"She didn't fall off and she wasn't kicked, but I don't know anything else because we rode after Sheila right away.

Logan gave the reins back to Beth and walked around the mare, feeling her legs.

"It seems as though she's okay," he said, and then he hesitated and crouched down so he could look at a spot on the horse's belly.

"Is there something wrong?" asked a worried Beth.

"Her legs are fine, but she has a swollen spot on her belly, right behind the girth."

"Huh?" Beth knelt down as well, and both Ricki and Kevin bent down from their saddles so they could see, too.

"Here!" Without touching the animal, Logan pointed at the swollen spot.

"What is that?"

He stood back up and shrugged his shoulders.

"Don't ask me. Maybe something stung her. If so, it must have really hurt. Look how swollen this is!"

Ricki and Kevin looked at each other.

"That would explain everything!"

Logan looked confused.

"What do you mean?"

"A bee sting would have really hurt her. That could

explain why Sheila took off so suddenly. After all, she's never done anything like that before. So she got a sting, or several, and then kicked at the bee. Marisa was startled, and Sheila too, obviously, so she took off!" Kevin said, and Ricki nodded.

"Exactly, that's how it seemed to me, too."

"Okay, now we have to figure out how to get her back home." Logan looked at Beth. "Should I ride her, or would you rather do it?"

"I ... I don't know," she admitted. She was still somewhat in shock. "It might be better if you did it. I'll ride your bike there and leave mine here; no one will take it with the flat tire. Maybe Carlotta would drive me back to get it."

Logan nodded. "I'm sure she will." He quickly adjusted the stirrups to fit him and then mounted Sheila with ease.

"See you later," he called to Beth and blew her a kiss.

"Be careful!" she shouted after him.

Kevin grinned.

"I think that gallop satisfied Diablo's and Sharazan's exercise needs," he joked, and then he and Ricki got their horses going again while Beth ran over to the bikes.

* * *

Patrick finally had calmed down, but a number of thoughts went through his mind.

Had it been a mistake to promise Marisa her own horse? Had he misjudged the dangers that riding and being around horses could bring? Would he ever be able to not worry when he knew that Marisa was out riding?

At the very least, it was clear to him that he was not going to buy Sheila for his daughter. However, it was also clear that he could not take back his promise of getting her a horse of her own. Marisa would always be disappointed in him if he did that.

He stole a glance at the girl in the back seat through the rearview mirror.

"We'll find another horse for you," he forced himself to say, but Marisa didn't even react.

Lost in her own thoughts, she stared out the window and tried to imagine what had happened to Sheila, and hoped the two riders had been able to catch her before she got hurt. They had driven all over the countryside but hadn't seen the riderless horse anywhere.

Suddenly, she seemed to awaken from a trance.

"Please, stop!" she begged her father, who obeyed immediately.

"Why? What's wrong? Are you sick?" he asked, worried.

"No!" She pointed through the window. "Look over there! Isn't that Sheila and two other horses?" she asked excitedly.

Mona squinted in order to see better.

"It's possible, but there's someone riding the brown horse."

"That's true." Disappointed, Marisa fell back against the seat. It couldn't be Sheila if there was someone in the saddle.

Slowly, Patrick started up the car again and concentrated on the road, while Mona and Marisa looked intently out the windows.

"Hey, stop!" Mona said all of a sudden, and put her hand on his arm.

"What? Again?"

"Just do it!"

As soon as the car stopped, Mona got out and looked at the girl on the bike, who had just ridden past them and was already a few yards further down the road in the other direction.

"Beth?" she called out hesitantly, and then a little louder. "BETH!"

The girl on the bike stopped, turned, and looked back in confusion, but then her face lit up and she turned her bike around.

"Aunt Mona! I'm so glad that I get to see you after all. I was just on my way to the ranch, hoping I could still catch you there."

In the meantime, Patrick and Marisa had gotten out of the car as well, and after they had all said their hellos, Beth said to her cousin, a little regretfully.

"The thing with Sheila didn't go well, did it?"

Amazed, the three Swintons looked at each other.

"How do you know that? You weren't even there."

"Well, my friends and I caught her and –"

"How is she? Is she okay?" Marisa wanted to know immediately.

"Yeah, she's fine. But I think she's going to be sore from that gallop."

Beth's cousin heaved a sigh of relief.

"I'm so glad nothing happened to her!"

"Ricki and Kevin are on their way to the ranch with Logan, my boyfriend, who's riding Sheila back. Actually, you must have seen them."

"Then I was right!"

Beth looked at her uncle. "What do you think of Sheila, apart from the fact that she ran off?" she asked, curious.

Patrick's facial expression became somber. "She bolted. That says it all, doesn't it?"

Beth immediately jumped to Sheila's defense.

"First of all, nothing happened, and secondly, Sheila couldn't help it if some stupid insect stung her."

Marisa wanted to hear exactly what had happened.

"I think you know more than we do," Mona said, "and we were there." The whole family listened closely as Beth explained.

After she had finished, Patrick felt embarrassed about his behavior toward Carlotta. "I think I'm going to have to apologize to Mrs. Mancini."

"And to Sheila!" Marisa was able to laugh again. She was so glad that nothing had happened to the horse.

"Come on," Patrick said to his niece. "Throw your bike in the trunk, and let's drive back to the ranch."

"Yes!" Marisa was happy. Carlotta would be glad to hear the good news that Sheila was okay, and the fact that Beth had confirmed that Sheila didn't have a mean bone in her body increased the chances of her getting the horse after all.

"Speaking of the bicycle, could we ..." began Beth, and right away, the Swintons' car rumbled down the field road so that she could pick up her bike as well.

* * *

Carlotta felt sad as she stood and stared off into the distance, waiting for the return of the two riders and hopefully of Sheila. Each minute her stomach cramped more, and she wondered for the hundredth time whether she should get in her car and drive toward them. However, since she had no idea where Sheila had gone, and the Swintons were already looking for her, she decided it didn't make any sense.

She walked in her halting steps back and forth across the yard and sent one prayer after another that at least the two riders would be safe.

Suddenly, she saw the Swintons' car on the road coming toward the ranch, approaching quickly.

Carlotta stared at it and swallowed nervously. She wondered if the family had found Sheila, and if they had, how she was. Were Ricki and Kevin all right?

So many questions flooded Carlotta's mind, and she hoped that in a few minutes the Swinton family would be able to answer them.

Chapter 9

The Swintons' car had barely stopped when Beth sprang out.

"Hey, Carlotta! I met up with my family after all. They drove me here. My bike had a flat tire and Logan is riding Sheila back. They should be here in about half an hour," she burst out.

Carlotta hesitated a moment, and then she grabbed the girl by both arms and stared at her, not quite sure she had heard correctly.

"What did you say, dear?"

"My bike had –"

"No, no, no! I meant about Sheila!" Carlotta interrupted.

"We caught her! Logan is riding her back here. Carlotta, I've gotta tell you, Ricki and Kevin rode like the wind and they drove Sheila directly into our arms. Then she stumbled and I was able to grab her reins. It was just like in the movies. I was scared to death!"

Carlotta swallowed.

"Sheila is okay?"

Beth could see how stressed Carlotta was, and she took both of Carlotta's hands in her own to reassure her.

"Yes, Carlotta, everything's okay. But Sheila does have a swollen spot on her belly from some kind of insect bite. Logan thought –"

"Bite?" Carlotta realized immediately what that meant.

Patrick stood behind her and coughed discreetly.

"Mrs. Mancini, I have to apologize to you for what I said. I was just so worried about my daughter," he explained.

Carlotta turned slowly to face him.

"I can understand that, Mr. Swinton. But I hope that you've come to realize that Sheila really isn't a mean horse. If she were, I never would have tried to sell her."

Patrick nodded, but before he could answer, Marisa burst out with a question that had been welling up in her during the whole drive back.

"Dad, if Sheila acted like that because of an insect bite, does that mean that we're going to buy her after all, in spite of everything that's happened?" she asked hopefully.

Patrick and Mona exchanged telling looks that seemed to indicate a silent agreement.

"Honestly, honey, we would rather buy you another horse. Insect bite or no, every time you went riding with her we would remember this incident all over again and it would make us very nervous."

"Oh!" Marisa looked disappointed. "And you would feel better if I were riding another horse, even though the same thing might happen again?"

Patrick nodded slowly.

"I know that sounds ridiculous, but it's a feeling I can't shake."

"I understand," answered Marisa, downhearted.

Mona looked back and forth between her husband and her daughter, and then she turned to Carlotta.

"Is Sheila the only horse you're selling?" she asked.

"Hmmm, at least she's the only horse that's one hundred percent healthy and not too old. The two ponies don't belong to me, and the others are getting on in years and are here to live out their lives peacefully."

Mona thought over what Carlotta had said.

"And tell me again how things are with Silver? You said he wouldn't have any problems if he weren't overworked, didn't you?"

Marisa's head jerked upward and her eyes began to shine again.

Silver! Given the situation with Sheila, she hadn't even thought about the gray horse.

Carlotta hesitated a moment.

"Silver? Yes, that's true, but joint damage is joint damage, and if Marisa wants to participate in tournaments, then –"

"I don't ride in tournaments!" Marisa objected. "I'd like to take a lesson a week, but no jumping, and besides that, I just want to go trail riding through the countryside."

"I see."

"And would Silver's joints be able to take that?" Mona asked directly.

"Well, that's hard to say. One never knows how joint problems will develop. If Marisa raced him every day the way Ricki and Kevin raced today, then Silver couldn't stand that for long, but on normal rides it shouldn't be a problem. But, as I said, I can't guarantee anything."

Mona nodded and observed Marisa, who was gazing longingly at Silver. She could sense exactly what her daughter was thinking.

"So would you perhaps be willing to sell Silver?"

"Well, I'd say we could talk about it, but maybe you should consider waiting a while and look for a completely healthy animal. After all, there's no hurry, and buying a horse isn't something that you should do hastily, just so you can say, 'Now I own a horse!' Marisa is a young girl who should be able to enjoy her horse for a long time. Maybe some day she'll want to ride competitively, and then Silver wouldn't be strong enough. Then you'd have to get a healthier horse."

During their conversation, Carlotta and her visitors, including Beth, walked over to the paddock, and while the adults were talking the girls ran out to the horses. Silver whinnied softly as he saw Marisa come toward him.

"Hey, you!" the girl greeted her dream horse and gave him an affectionate hug around his muscular neck, pressing close to him.

Beth watched her thoughtfully.

"Can I tell you something? Silver suits you a lot better."

Marisa sighed. "Tell that to Carlotta."

"I don't have to tell her. I'm sure she can see that herself."

Beth was right. Carlotta had been observing Marisa carefully, as had her parents. Slowly a smile spread across her face and she placed a gentle hand on Mona's shoulder.

"I have the feeling that you and Marisa have both decided on Silver, no matter what I say. That's true, isn't it?"

Marisa's mother turned and a faint blush colored her cheeks. "I saw a spark between my daughter and Silver from the beginning," she confessed, "but she needed to be aware of it, too."

"It's wonderful when the whole family loves an animal, but in my honest opinion, Marisa would be much better off with a stronger horse."

Mona sighed. "I know. But sick horses have as much right to a loving home as healthy ones, even though they can only be ridden within limits, or not at all."

"That's true, and it's a nice thought, but what would you do, for example, if Silver couldn't be ridden after five years? Would you get your daughter a second horse and keep Silver as a companion horse or would you get rid of the poor guy? After all, not everyone can afford two horses. You see, there are basic issues that we have to consider first."

Patrick nodded and was just about to add his comments when he and the women heard the girls out on the paddock laughing loudly, and turned to see what was going on.

Beth and Marisa were walking back to join the adults, and Silver kept following them and poking his head against Marisa's back.

"He is so adorable!" Marisa called out. "So affectionate and – oh, I don't know how to describe it – he's just completely different from Sheila. I mean, she's a wonderful horse, but he ... he's just special!"

Carlotta heart warmed at Marisa's description of the gray gelding.

"Every horse is special," she replied, and after a short pause, she asked, "Would you like to ride him?"

Marisa's eyes shone.

"Oh, yes, please!"

"All right, then. Beth will show you where the saddles are."

Marisa led Silver off the paddock happily and brought him to the stable, followed by her cousin.

"I would only sell Silver with a protective clause in the contract," Carlotta said suddenly. "I want to make sure that he would be returned to Mercy Ranch if you decide to get another horse some day."

"That would be fine, but we don't intend to get rid of our horse after we take him home. Marisa would be furious, for starters!" laughed Patrick. "But let's see what our daughter says after she gets back from her ride."

Carlotta nodded and glanced around. When she saw what was coming up the road, her face lit up.

"Oh, they're back. I'm so relieved! Please, excuse me!" She walked toward the riders.

"Oh, my dears, I don't know how to thank you!" she called out, and wrapped her arms around Sheila. "That could have ended tragically."

"It was a terrific ride!" grinned Kevin and winked at Carlotta. "Ricki's decided to become a jockey."

"Never!" the girl swore to that in front of witnesses, and she was just about to dismount when Marisa led Silver out of the stable and toward the riding ring.

"Oh, no, I think I'd better stay in the saddle," she exclaimed, but Carlotta shook a finger at her. "Don't even suggest such a thing! Get down right now!" she laughed. After she inspected the insect bite on Sheila's belly she asked Logan to take her into the stable and apply an ointment that would ease the swelling and the itch. She wanted to stay close to Marisa in case anything went wrong.

* * *

Marisa rode for forty-five minutes before jumping down from the saddle.

"I love him!" was her only comment after giving the animal with the gentle eyes an enthusiastic kiss on his nose.

"And you could imagine being happy with him?" asked Carlotta. "Even with the limitations on riding him?"

Marisa nodded.

"Oh, yes!" she said, without even thinking about it, and then she looked at her parents anxiously.

'Pleeeeeease!' her lips formed the word silently. After a few seconds of thought, which seemed endless to Marisa, Patrick finally said, "Then I would say the I.O.U. is cashed in."

"Yeah!" Marisa gave an exuberant shout and hugged her horse warmly. Her horse! The most wonderful creature in the whole world: HER HORSE! She would never give him away, even if there came a day when he could no longer be ridden. This animal had won her heart, and she would do everything to make sure that Silver was happy for the rest of his life.

"Marisa, I'm so happy for you!" Beth gave her cousin a hug. "And, of course, for Silver, too! You know, boy, that you couldn't have found a better home!"

Ricki and Kevin came over, too, to offer congratulations, and a few moments later they were joined by Logan.

"Are you celebrating something?" he asked, laughing, when he saw Marisa's beaming smile.

"You could say that! Sodas for everyone!" Beth called out, and then she hurried off to get the drinks while the adults went into Carlotta's office to sign the bill of sale.

"I didn't know I could be this happy!" announced Marisa, who couldn't stop looking at her Silver.

"Hah, I could have told you that before, but you never asked me!" joked Beth, and poked her cousin in the ribs.

Ricki, whose throat was so dry, drank a cola almost in one gulp. She looked pensively at Marisa and then said, "I think I know someone else who will be just as happy as you that you chose Silver."

Beth, Kevin, and Logan looked at each other, nodding in the shared unspoken knowledge, but Marisa hadn't the slightest clue what was going on.

"What do you mean by that?" she asked, puzzled.

"She means Cheryl," Beth answered for Ricki. "She's going to be so thrilled when she finds out her foster horse is staying right here!"

"Oh," laughed Marisa. "Then say hi to her from me, and tell her I was happy to do this for her."

"Liar!" grinned Beth. "If you could decide right now between Silver and Sheila, without anyone trying to persuade you, who would you choose?"

"Silver!" exclaimed Marisa spontaneously, and stroked her gelding across the forehead.

"Okay, you passed the test," responded Beth.

"How about unsaddling him now? Then we could take him and Sheila out onto the paddock for a while," Logan suggested.

Marisa thought that was a good idea.

"Okay. I'm sure he wants to say good-bye to his stable companions. After all, he's not going to be here much longer. I think I'm going to take him home this week."

As the friends walked back to the stable with Silver, Kevin whispered to Ricki, "Marisa is really nice!"

Ricki gave him a teasing look. "Even though you're right, I didn't need to hear that!"

* * *

The kids had decided not to tell Cheryl anything, and so the next day during lunch break Cheryl sat on a bench and stared straight ahead, not participating in any conversation with her classmates.

Suddenly Beth walked up to her.

"Hello," she began, a little shyly. Cheryl looked away from her.

"Leave me alone!" she answered wearily.

"I want to talk to you."

"But I don't want to talk with you."

"Okay, that was pretty direct."

"It was supposed to be!"

Beth put her hands on her hips. "You're acting like a little kid! I thought we were friends."

Cheryl looked at her angrily. "Yeah, that's what I used to think!"

"Cheryl, it's not going to change anything about Sheila, no matter how mad you are at me."

"Yeah, but it might not have gone this far if you hadn't dragged your cousin into this!"

"Oh, I wouldn't say that," answered Beth vaguely.

"Please, I don't want to talk to you right now," said Cheryl a second time, and she got up and went to sit on a bench further away.

"Well, then don't!" called Beth after her, but she thought to herself: *I'm pretty sure that you will want to soon!* Turning in the opposite direction, she ran back to Logan, who was standing with the others a few yards away.

Ricki was just telling Lillian and Cathy what had happened to Sheila, and they were hanging on her every word.

"Drat, the one time something exciting happens, and we're not there," Lillian responded, and exchanged glances with Cathy.

"That's so true," said Cathy. "You guys had a real adventure, and I had to survive an afternoon birthday party for my aunt. Life is so unfair!"

"I'm sorry if I'm interrupting," commented Beth, joining the group. "Cheryl's still furious at me. I don't think I'll ever get her to ride out to the ranch again."

"Wait a minute." Ricki reached into her jeans pocket. "I forgot all about this!" She pulled out Cheryl's key ring and grinned. "Another reason to talk to her. I'll see if I have any luck." Ricki casually walked over to Cheryl, who was now staring into space.

"Are you guys all in on this together?" Cheryl asked almost indifferently as soon as Ricki came up to her. "Are you all trying to take turns cheering me up? It isn't necessary. I'll be okay."

"That's great that you're okay," Ricki said amicably. "Actually, I just wanted to give you this." She held out the key ring.

"Where did you get that?" a surprised Cheryl asked as she took it. "I was looking all over for it. Thanks!"

"I found it at the lake."

"Oh."

Ricki waited a moment to see if her friend would say anything else, but she remained silent.

"Carlotta is getting a hay delivery today. Can you come and help?"

Cheryl shook her head.

"Why not?" Ricki wouldn't leave it alone.

"That's a stupid question!"

"Hey, you know that Carlotta needs all the help she can get."

"I know, but I can't. Don't you understand that? I just can't go into the stable! It would drive me crazy to see Sheila's empty stall." Cheryl replied sadly.

"So you're not going to help Carlotta because of an empty stall? I think that's dumb! Not just dumb, but selfish!" Ricki shot back. "Look, there are other horses at Mercy Ranch that Carlotta works her tail off for! Have you forgotten that? It's called Mercy Ranch. *Mercy Ranch*! A home for neglected horses! And just because there's an empty stall there now doesn't mean that we can just fold our hands in our laps and do nothing. These horses need our help. And they need hay. And in order to get it to them we have to unload it. Do you understand that?"

As was her habit, Ricki was all passion when she fought for something she believed in. And she wasn't going to let Cheryl off easily by allowing her to feel sorry for herself.

"If you love horses as much as you say you do, then do what you can to help them. I know that the thing with Sheila is hard for you. I'd feel the same way, but still ... even if you're mad at Carlotta, the horses shouldn't have to suffer. So help us this afternoon, please! And anyway, just sitting around and thinking about it isn't going to change a thing. Distraction is the best medicine. Think about it! Oh, and the hay wagon will be there around three-thirty."

With these words, Ricki walked off and rejoined the

others. She didn't know if she had been able to convince Cheryl to go to Mercy Ranch or not.

"There's only one thing we can do now," she said to her friends. "Wait and see."

***

As the clock struck 3:00 Cheryl was already on her way to Mercy Ranch.

Earlier that afternoon, when she got home from school, she finally had the long overdue talk with her mother, and then she sat in her room for a while thinking over what Ricki had said. On her desk was the poem she had written the day before. She picked it up and reread a few of the lines:

... Nevertheless,
I'll keep waiting
In the hope
That one day
My tears will stop,
That one day
My heart will laugh again
And I will be able
To free myself
From the valley of tears
So that I can rise up
To a new happiness ...

"'... rise up to new happiness ...' If I keep sitting around here, nothing is going to get better," she murmured to herself. Ricki was right. Maybe she should distract herself. And when she thought of Silver, Hadrian, Jonah, and all the others, she began to feel guilty.

She stood up, determined. She knew it would hurt to see Sheila's empty stall, but so what if she had promised herself never to go into a stable again. She knew now that it would hurt her even more to live without horses. Even though Sheila wouldn't be there anymore, the others would greet her and blow air into her hair playfully, just as Sheila had.

"The most important thing is that you keep Sheila in your heart, in your memory, and that you remain thankful for the time you had to spend with her," her mother had said. "You'll never forget Sheila, but your life will go on, and you will get to know a lot of other horses that you will fall in love with, too!"

***

Cheryl had almost reached Mercy Ranch when she saw Carlotta's horses on the paddock. Her heart contracted painfully as she realized that Sheila wasn't one of them anymore.

She was almost tempted to turn around, but she vowed not to get teary, so she clenched her teeth and pedaled furiously until she got there. She just had to force herself to stop thinking about Sheila.

All of her friends sat lazily against the ranch house wall sunning themselves when Cheryl arrived.

"Hi," said Lillian, and the others greeted her as if they had never doubted that she would come back.

"Hey!" she greeted them back and then sat down next to Ricki.

"I knew you'd come."

"How did you know?"

"Because if I had been you, I would have come," answered Ricki softly.

"The hay hasn't come yet, has it?"

Kevin shook his head.

"No! Oh, by the way, you're supposed to go see Carlotta. I almost forgot."

"Why?"

"I have no idea."

Cheryl got up a little nervously and opened the door to the house.

"Oh, Cheryl, there you are!" Carlotta was truly happy to see the girl. "Well, let's get right to the point. There's a new arrival in the stable, and I thought, after what happened ... Anyway, I thought it would be good for you, and also for the horse, to spend some time together."

Cheryl swallowed.

"I don't know if I can yet," she replied slowly.

"Hmm, I thought you might say that, so here's what I suggest. Just try it, and if you find that you can't do it yet, then you can tell me, and I'll ask Bev to take the animal on. Is that all right with you?"

The girl nodded.

"Good!" Carlotta smiled. "Then go on out and try your luck."

Cheryl got up and left the office. Slowly she walked across the hallway to the connecting door between the stable and the house. However, as her hand rested on the doorknob, she hesitated. She was afraid that she would betray Sheila if she became attached to this new horse.

Cheryl struggled with herself for a few minutes until she heard Carlotta's voice encouraging her, "Go on!"

Finally, she managed to overcome her fears and walk

into the stable, her eyes downcast. She didn't want to see Sheila's empty stall.

Almost immediately, she was startled by a familiar greeting whinny.

No! something shouted inside Cheryl. *I must be crazy! It can't be! That's just totally impossible!* Then she looked up and stared at her darling foster horse, who was stretching out her head as far as possible over the stall's half door toward her.

"Sheila!" Cheryl's voice cracked, and she felt as if the floor beneath her had been pulled away. Her eyes wide, she stared at Sheila as if she were a ghost.

"What are you waiting for?" asked Carlotta softly. She had come in behind her unnoticed and now she gave Cheryl a gentle push in the back, jerking her back to reality.

She looked at Carlotta in disbelief, and then ran over to the stall, opened the door with shaking hands, and wrapped herself around Sheila's neck.

Tears ran down her cheeks as she buried her face in the mare's thick mane. Laughing and sobbing at once, she waded through a sea of feelings. Even when she saw all her friends gathered in front of the stall, she was not ashamed of her tears.

"Well? Isn't that a wonderful hay delivery?" asked Ricki and winked at her. "It would have been too bad if you hadn't come to help unload it, wouldn't it?"

"You ... you knew, didn't you? You all knew and no one told me. Oh, how mean can you be?" Cheryl wiped the tears from her eyes and couldn't believe how happy she was.

"And Sheila? She's staying here? I mean, forever?" she

asked Carlotta, hopefully. "I don't know if I can bear losing her a second time!"

Carlotta nodded.

"I wanted to sell a horse and I did. Marisa decided on Silver, so Sheila will stay here, unless you buy her some day and board her somewhere else."

Cheryl tried not to shout out her joy. "I'm so happy! You can't imagine! Oh, by the way, could someone take a picture of Sheila? I cut up all the ones I had. I'm such an idiot!"

Her friends laughed and Logan pulled out his camera phone.

"No problem!" he said, and he pressed the button, taking a picture of Cheryl, her eyes red from crying, but happy, beside her horse.

"So now it's time for Sheila to go back out to the paddock with the other horses. We kept her in the stable just for you," said Carlotta, and while Cheryl led the animal out of the stable, Kevin asked, "Did you hear that Diablo, Sharazan, and Sheila ran a race yesterday? And did you hear that Beth caught Sheila when she bolted?"

"What?" Confused, Cheryl looked at Ricki's boyfriend.

"Yeah, you missed a lot yesterday," he said.

As Sheila galloped across the meadow to join her stable companions, Cheryl made the others tell her everything.

She listened wide-eyed, and when Kevin finished she turned to Beth, feeling pretty embarrassed.

"I'm grateful to you for catching Sheila," she said with a grin. "And I'm sorry that I was so mad at you."

Beth gave her a hug. "Well, catching her wasn't that big a deal. We all worked together, and it was more of a coincidence that I was able to grab Sheila's reins."

"You know what? It doesn't matter anymore. The important thing is that she's okay, and that she's going to stay here," said Cheryl, overjoyed.

Ricki nudged Kevin, laughing.

"Hey, it looks as if you're going to have to ride Sharazan yourself, after all, at the Fun and Games Tournament," she teased.

Her boyfriend groaned dramatically.

"What Fun and Games Tournament? What's that?" Cheryl, who had been completely in the dark about the event, listened as Ricki briefly explained to her what is was all about.

"If Carlotta doesn't mind, I'm going to register Sheila and me, too!" announced the girl, impulsively.

"I don't know what you guys like about dunking your head in a bucket of water," Kevin shook himself like a wet cat.

"You just don't want to play because you're afraid you won't win," Lillian accused him.

"Exactly!" agreed Cathy, and even Ricki nodded emphatically.

"That's right!"

"Not a chance against the girls!"

"Just a scaredy-cat!"

"Enough!" Kevin stood up. "If you girls think I'm going to let you say that about me, then you're going to be surprised. Starting tomorrow, I'm going to train until I drop!"

Ricki gave him a thumbs-up.

"I knew you wouldn't let us think that about you. Welcome to the club of the unbeatable Fun and Games Festival riders!" she laughed. "Girls, you all heard him! Kevin wants to train tomorrow, so we don't want to miss that!"

And so it was that the next day, Kevin, on Sharazan, under the eagle eyes – and laughter – of Ricki, Lillian, Cathy, Cheryl, Beth, and Logan, rode from one bucket of water to the next, missing every apple he bobbed for and swallowing a great deal of water in the attempt. By the evening, the boy couldn't stand to even look at an apple.

Exhausted from his labors, he didn't have enough energy left to eat dinner that night. Instead, he went straight to his room, where fifteen minutes later he was fast asleep with all his clothes still on, dreaming that a huge apple sat on Sharazan and rode slalom through a row of enormous buckets in which his friends sat jeering.

Awakened from his nightmare, Kevin swore he'd never again train for another Fun and Games Festival, no matter how many times Ricki called him "scaredy-cat!"

Also by author Gabi Adam:

Diablo – My Dream Horse

Diablo – To the Rescue

A New Home for Diablo

Worried About Diablo

Hero of the Night

Last Chance for Golden Star

Diablo's Double!

Diablo – The Bequest

Diablo – The Secret of Echo Lake

Diablo – Race Against Time

Diablo – A Day Like Any Other

Diablo – Freed From Fear

Diablo – The Test of Courage

Diablo – Days of Darkness

Diablo – The New Girl

Trouble at Mercy Ranch